Ten Rules of Youth Ministry

AND WHY ONEIGHTY® BREAKS THEM ALL

by

Blaine Bartel

Harrison House
Tulsa, Oklahoma

06 05 04 03 02   10 9 8 7 6 5 4 3 2

Ten Rules of Youth Ministry and Why Oneighty® Breaks Them All
ISBN 1-57794-426-7
Copyright © 2002 by Blaine Bartel
PO Box 691923
Tulsa, Oklahoma 74179

Published by Harrison House, Inc.
P.O. Box 35035
Tulsa, Oklahoma 74153

contents

i acknowledge

In the spirit of "less is more," a bedrock principle we endeavor to live by at Oneighty®, I am incredibly grateful to the following people:

- Mom and Dad - I want to be just like you

- Pastor Willie and Deleva George - for believing in a Canadian

- My brother Jason, my sister Luanne - for putting up with me

- Ken and Trudi Blount - for your prayers, your support

- Erik Lawson - my partner in crime-fighting

- Whit George - for making me think

- Lee Wilson - I have never been more proud of anyone

- My Oneighty® staff - simply the best

- Church On The Move coworkers and congregation – it is an honor to serve with you

- Ron and Katie Luce - for true friendship

- Tommy and Rachel Burchfield - you love, you inspire

- Josh McDowell - my model, my colleague, you raised the bar for all of us

- Dave, Joyce, and Danny Meyer – real people who really care

- Pastors everywhere - for 20 years of trusting me with your sheep

- Grady Williams and Gordie Lagore - my youth Pastors

- Dave Lagore - my first Pastor

- Rosie, Stu - for showing me Christ

- Jesus - for showing me mercy

- and last, but in no way any less, Keith Provance and all my new friends at Harrison House

i dedicate

this book to

Cathy, my closest companion,

and

Jeremy, Dillon, and Brock,

my best friends.

introduction

The last six years have been a blur to say the least. I often sit back and ask God why He chose me of all people. This amazing journey began in a place I never thought I'd leave. I was the pastor of a growing church in Colorado Springs when I received a phone call from my pastor and spiritual mentor, Willie George. He had an obvious air of excitement in his voice as he told me about this new youth ministry, one he was developing and leading.

What? A senior pastor excited about youth ministry? I had to hear this. His associate pastor was actually preaching his mid-week service so he could be with the teenagers. He had taken his nationally syndicated television program off the air and used those funds for his local youth ministry. *You've got to be kidding!* I thought.

He asked me to come and preach for him. I was introduced to a way of youth ministry that I'd never seen before. It was called Oneighty®. A teenager in the group had come up with the name. It stood for repentance, but I'm quite sure most unsuspecting students that came for the first time thought it was an "x-games" concept. I came in, preached, and the traditions of youth ministry were over for me. It should be done this way.

This kind of youth ministry had been a dream, until this moment in my life. I had always thought I was on the cutting edge, but this was beyond any of the edges I had ever seen. It was a whole new mountain, and the view was breathtaking! I had discovered a pastor who was ready to commit time, people, and money to impact a city's teenagers. He wasn't just talking a good game, but had stepped up to the plate and was swinging for the fence.

When I arrived at the church I had helped start more than ten years before, I found a completely remodeled youth room. It looked like something you might see on MTV. The group had mushroomed from a couple hundred kids to over 500 in just a matter of months. It wasn't just the room. I saw an army of young people responding to a pastor they knew really cared about them. For the first time, they were proud of their youth group. You didn't have to beg them to bring their friends each week. They just did.

Then the question came. I knew it was coming and I already knew the answer. "Yes." A huge "YES!" I had to be part of this. My wife and I resigned from our church and moved back to Tulsa. In the six years that followed, Oneighty® continued to explode; we conducted multiple services to handle the thousands of students who would come week after week. Some even came from outside the state of Oklahoma every week just to be part of it.

I have always been one to go against the tide and break rules that deserve to be broken. People who break the right rules earn the opportunity to change the world.

I have enjoyed over 20 years of full-time youth ministry, and I am sure I have seen it all. Unfortunately, I have seen a lot of youth ministers and ministries come and go. I have watched helplessly as young ministers were destroyed by their own mistakes. I saw my own youth pastor push and strive to the point of a nervous breakdown, putting him in the hospital and completely out of ministry for years.

It doesn't have to be that hard. We must quit trying to cut down this oak tree with an old, rusty, dull axe. I believe the truth, principles, and strategies you receive from this book will sharpen your ability to compel today's teenager to live for Jesus Christ.

This is not a book about how wonderful Oneighty® has become. It is about how wonderful your youth ministry can become. I want to help you succeed and give you tools to grow. And you will, but you must break some rules.

- As a rule, pastors today aren't that involved in their youth groups.

- As a rule, youth pastors don't work well with their pastors.

- As a rule, churches don't spend a lot of money on their teenagers.

- As a rule, unchurched students don't like church.

- As a rule, youth leaders do not command much respect in their congregations.

- As a rule, church youth groups are virtually ignored by their communities.

- As a rule, reading a book isn't likely to make any major difference in your future.

It's time to break the rules.

Blaine Bartel

why break the rules?

DEVELOP NEW METHODS TO REACH YOUNG PEOPLE

Contrary to what you might think, youth ministry, as we know it, did not begin in the church. It emerged in the mid-1940s out of a growing evangelistic movement in the United States. Young, vibrant ministers held rallies across the country toward the close of World War II in an effort to reach the youth of our nation who were not being reached through normal church channels.

In an effort to organize this growing movement, ministries like Youth for Christ were born. Only after pastors witnessed the outstanding success of crusades did they embrace youth ministry and introduce its revolutionary methods into their local churches. Pastors then hired these same itinerant evangelists to head up their newly created youth programs. Thus began the ministry of "youth pastors."

Youth ministry across the United States has radically evolved since the forties and fifties. It has grown with the changing culture of each generation. There are some long-held rules still used in our churches today that I believe need to be broken. When we analyze the results, it is evident these laws do not work.

Thom S. Rainer, Dean of the Billy Graham School of Evangelism and Missions, wrote the book *The Bridger Generation.* This valuable tool should be in every youth leader and minister's library. From it you will learn how to deal with the teenagers who go to your church and, more importantly, those who do not go to your church. You will gain insight into what today's young people believe and how they think. Until you grasp their thoughts and beliefs, you will not know how to effectively minister to them.

In his book, Rainer documents the percentages of teenagers who have come to the Lord since the early 1900s.

- The Builder generation: Born between 1910 and 1946.[1] Sixty-five percent were reached for Christ in their teens.[2]

- The Boomer generation: Born between 1947 and 1964.[3] Thirty-five percent of the youth of that day were won to the Lord.[4]

- The Buster generation: Born between 1965 and 1976.[5] Fifteen percent gave their hearts to the Lord.[6]

- The Bridger generation: Born between 1977 and 1994.[7] Only four percent of all Bridgers have been reached for Christ.[8]

It is obvious from the statistics that we are not doing our job. Most churches across America have a youth pastor on staff. Yet, we are not successful in reaching the young people in our churches or the "unchurched" kids in our communities. *Campus Life* magazine recently surveyed teenagers and found 88 percent do not attend church regularly. Of the 12 percent that do, 88 percent plan to stop attending once they graduate from high school.[9]

In 1999 it was reported that 10,000 churches did not have any conversions among their young people.[10] They could not have had much going on in their youth ministry because teens are easy to convert. Young people are hungry, and they are searching. This leads me to believe the fault lies with ministers who adhere to techniques that worked well with one generation but miserably fail today. If we would only take the time to find out what is relevant among kids today and tailor our methods and message accordingly, we would see a dramatic increase in the number of Bridgers accepting Jesus as their Savior.

Improvement should also be made in the area of church leadership. Most pastors have failed to invest the proper time and money to train their staff to be effective. I am sure many of the youth ministers began their ministry as I did. My pastor in Calgary, Canada, where I grew up, approached me and said, "You look like you're good with kids, and we really need your help." I was then thrown into the middle of a bunch of teens and told to do a good job.

All too often workers start out with little or no training. They are half-afraid of the kids and focus on keeping them out of trouble rather than mobilizing them to reach their generation. It is time to change!

Who Made These Rules?

I have read some amusing articles in newspapers where a person was fined or arrested for breaking a blue law. Blue laws regulate private and public conduct. While most have been removed from the law books, some states retain these regulations today. I call them "Looney Laws," and they really need to be thrown out!

For instance, in Wilbur, Washington, it is illegal to ride an ugly horse down the street. If you happen to fly over the state of Maine and decide you would like to step out of the airplane, you will be arrested after they pick up your splattered body off the ground! It is illegal to carry an ice cream cone in your pocket in Lexington, Kentucky. I am sure you are wondering how these rules were ever made in the first place and why they are still in existence.

Likewise, it is time to examine some of the outdated laws of youth ministry. Some of these rules need to be broken if we are to be effective in reaching the Bridger generation.

Law vs. Truth

There is a difference between a rule and a truth. For every rule I am committed to break, I will give you a truth that I am dedicated to keep. A *rule* is an established standard or habit of behavior. A **truth** is a scientific law that is fixed by basic principle.

Let's examine two rules. One was followed in the Old Testament. If it had been broken, a nation of people would not have languished in a desert until the "rule keepers" died. The other rule affects us today. It was challenged and broken. Consequently, one man changed the way an entire industry operates.

We will begin with Moses. He commissioned twelve men, one from each tribe of Israel, to spy out the Promised Land. (Num. 13:25-33.) When the spies returned, only two of them believed they could go in and take possession of the land of Canaan. The other ten men looked at the strong giants and the walled cities and would not break the law found in verse 31. It says, "We be not able to go up against the people; for they are stronger than we." They believed the old rule: If someone is bigger than you are, you lose.

God promised the children of Israel He would give the land to them. (Lev. 20:24.) Caleb tried to echo the promise when he said, "Let us go up at once, and possess [the land]; for we are well able to overcome it" (Num. 13:30).

Remember this: Principles believed followed by actions taken will always supersede rules men have made. If the Israelites had believed the promise, the principle of God's Word would have gone into action. The rule says, "They are bigger, so we cannot win," but the principle says, "We can have whatever God has spoken even if it looks impossible." If only they had followed the truth rather than the rule, they would not have needlessly wondered in the wilderness for forty years.

Revolutionary Ideas

The second rule was challenged in the mid-seventies. It was an unbroken rule in the restaurant industry, which remained intact until a man came along with an idea that forever changed the way food was served. He worked for the McDonald's Corporation. He believed his idea would cause the business to flourish and sell more hamburgers than ever before. He was not in management; in fact, he had a lower-level position in the company.

He called a meeting with a group of executives to present his revolutionary theory. It was very simple: put in a large window on the side of the building. Customers could then drive to the window and pick up their food without getting out of their cars.

The executives looked at him as though he had lost his mind. The rule was that Americans wanted to sit down in a nice restaurant to have dinner with their families. People do not eat and drive at the same time.

However, he was persistent, and month after month he presented different variations of his proposal, hoping the McDonald's management team would grasp the idea. They were convinced it was a stupid plan, but because of his persistence, they finally agreed to try his wacky idea in one franchise, with the promise he would leave them alone once it was evident the idea was a bad one.

You know the rest of the story. Once they began serving hamburgers through this window, business exploded. Today you find few fast-food restaurants without a drive-through window. His "bad" idea has even been implemented by other industries as well. Banks, pharmacies, and dry cleaners utilize his radical concept!

It should be noted that McDonald's did not change their menu. They still sold hamburgers but changed their method of delivery. Our menu is the gospel message, and it continues to stand the test of time. It is still good news to today's teenager!

Thinking Outside the Box

I believe there are "drive-through window" ideas for today's youth ministry, but it requires us to step outside the walls and expand the borders. We need to come up with new ideas and methods on how to reach teenagers. Revolutionary ideas and cutting-edge methods are out there just waiting for someone to discover them.

We are not trying to change the gospel. That has to stay the same. You cannot change the message of the Cross and Resurrection because it is our foundation. While it will never change, the methodology has to constantly evolve with every culture. The gospel message must be placed in an attractive package to reach this generation of young people and catch their attention.

We live in a time where packaging is of the utmost importance. The outside container is just as important as the contents to consumers. When a person shops to buy a dress shirt, he will pick up one that is packaged nicely. He will pull off the cellophane wrap to get a better look at the shirt. Once he checks it out and decides the shirt looks pretty good, he will put the opened package back on the shelf and take a shirt that is in an unopened package!

Teenagers are the same way. The gospel has to be delivered in a culturally cool package, or they will not bother to listen to what you have to say. We are ministering to a group of carnal kids who have been influenced by music videos, slick advertising, television, and movies. If we do not present the gospel in an equally appealing way, our youth will continue to be drawn away by the world's influence.

Only four out of every one hundred kids under the age of twenty have given their lives to the Lord. A four-percent minority is unacceptable. It is time for us to change the paradigm and emerge from the rules that have restricted us from truly reaching today's youth.

TOUGH QUESTIONS

Q: Blaine, how did you get started in youth ministry?

A: I feel like I've been in youth ministry since I was saved. I received Christ when I was 16 years old in a revival of sorts in my high school. A friend of mine led me to Christ and I have been working with young people ever since.

It all started with reaching my peers and leading friends in my school to Christ. After high school I went to *Youth With A Mission* because I wanted to learn what ministry was all about, how to do it, and I wanted to grow my own relationship with Christ. At *Youth With A Mission* I had the privilege of serving under John Dawson, who was our base leader. I learned a lot about evangelism, missions, and relevant ways of reaching young people and the youth culture. I spent a year there, then came back and served in my local church. I was faithful working in the children's ministry and the youth ministry.

During that time I met the man who would become the spiritual mentor in my life, Pastor Willie George. I met him at a conference he conducted at our church in Calgary, Alberta, Canada.

He said, "Blaine if you ever go to Bible school in Tulsa, look me up. I'd love to put you to work in our ministry if you're ever in the city."

About four months later we were there. My wife, Cathy, and I went to Bible school and we began to serve with Pastor George. We have now been with him in ministry for more than 20 years. With his ministry we were able to launch "Fire by Nite," a television program we did for many, many years, reaching young people nationally and internationally in youth groups.

I have worked with Pastor George at Church On The Move with the Oneighty® program for the last six years. We have seen it grow and many young people come to Christ.

I have been in youth ministry a long time and it has been an incredible journey. It is a journey I would not trade for anything.

Q: You've served more than 20 years in full-time youth ministry. How are we doing today?

A: I think we are doing better than we have ever done, but I know we have a long way to go. It is interesting; I've done a reverse of most people in youth ministry who have been in it for 20 years. I started out traveling and itinerating. In the first 12 years of our ministry, I held crusades, conferences, and training events, and I did outside ministry beyond the local church.

I had small stints where I was the youth pastor. After that I was a pastor for four years and learned the role of the senior pastor. We raised a church in Colorado Springs from three families to about 500 people, and after four years my pastor, Willie George, called us and asked if we would come back and help him with Oneighty®. That was just beginning.

Today, I see everything coming back to the local church. We can have great concerts, conferences, and national events, but if we're not reaching young people week in and week out through our local churches, we're really not being effective. That is where my heart is. My heart is in reaching our kids at Church On The Move and then helping other youth leaders across the country and around the world reach young people in their local church.

We are seeing great progress. Most importantly, pastors today are taking up the mantle of youth ministry and making a commitment to their local church youth group.

Q: Who have been the greatest influences in your ministry?

A: Without a doubt, my own wife and children have been great influences. My wife is committed. She has supported me and kept me honest. My wonderful mom and dad constantly pray for me and encourage me through thick and thin, and there have been good times and difficult times.

My pastor has provided a model of integrity for me, the importance of staying true to the Word of God for excellence in all we do. He has probably been the greatest spiritual influence in my life.

John Dawson and **Youth With A Mission** was important to me early on in my ministry. They helped me develop a real commitment to Christ and a fervor for evangelism.

Ron Luce has been a good friend and a great influence in my life. Proverbs 27:17 says that iron sharpens iron, and Ron and I have been sharpening each other for 15 years now. Josh McDowell is and has been an incredible influence. He was a model for me as a younger minister. Watching how he leads, how he teaches, and the commitment he has made shows me I can keep going as he keeps going.

My good friend Whit George, Pastor George's son, has been an incredible influence in the area of understanding youth culture. There have been others like Tommy Burchfield, Ken Blount, Erik Lawson, Lee Wilson, and of course, Wayne Gretzky and U2.

rule one:

convince your pastor to get behind your vision

Traditionally, pastors have divorced themselves from youth ministry. All too often, they will pour their heart and soul into other areas of the church—Sunday services, missions, or the church facility. For some reason, they hand the teenagers over to the youth pastor. The attitude has been, "Keep those kids out of my hair!" Pastors will find a room for the youth to meet, usually as far away from the sanctuary as possible. They do not want their service disrupted. Typically, the mandate to the youth pastor is "Just try to get them to a place where they are not having sex or taking drugs."

Unfortunately, because of this attitude, many youth pastors have followed the first time-honored rule that needs to be broken.

Rule One: *Convince your pastor to get behind your vision.*

A problem develops in local churches when youth ministers try to convert the pastor to their vision. It *has* to be the other way around. Therefore, this rule needs to be replaced with the following truth.

Truth One: *A truly effective youth ministry must be pastor-driven.*

Youth pastors should grab hold of their pastor's vision and reflect his dream and passion in their ministry to the youth. Only then will they put themselves in a position to have the full support of their pastor and ultimately the support of the true head of the church, the Lord Jesus.

Everyone is rooted in Christ, but the pastor is the trunk of the tree out of which all elements of ministry must flow. Jesus placed only one head in each local church body. Youth pastors are under-shepherds and operate with delegated authority. Therefore, all youth ministry must align itself with the pastor's vision. If a youth minister tries to operate under his own authority, his department will end up having a different flavor or characteristics than the rest of the church.

God never intended for the senior pastor to go in one direction, while the youth minister heads somewhere else, and then the children's department arrives in yet a third direction. He wants each local body moving together with synergy, unity, and oneness. The church's vision can only start with the pastor. It is his responsibility to hear from God and effectively communicate his vision to each ministry department in his church.

Turning Hearts

We are living in the final days before the return of the Lord Jesus Christ. Because of the time in which we live, God is doing a powerful work in families. Malachi 4:6 says God "shall turn the heart of the fathers to the children, and the heart of the children to their fathers." Ministries like Promise Keepers and Ed Cole's Christian Men's Network have made an impact in encouraging men to take their place as the head of their home, both spiritually and naturally. We are seeing a real change in the lives of fathers making an investment in their families.

I believe God is also speaking to spiritual fathers—to the pastors and bishops—and is turning their hearts back to the young people in their churches and communities. The Scripture in Malachi points out that when this happens, there will be an incredible turning of teenagers back to their fathers or back to the church.

Before Jesus ascended into heaven, He said to Peter, "I want you to feed my lambs." (John 21:15.) He then told him to feed His sheep. (vv. 16,17.) Peter did not know it at the time, but he was appointed the early church's first pastor. His first instructions from Jesus were to go after the young people. His job was to raise up the lambs and guide them so they would grow in the Lord. Once taught and trained by their pastor, they in turn would be used to affect the lives of others.

The Pastor's Commitment

As the pastor turns his heart to the teenagers, there are three important resources he must commit himself to if he wants to see the hearts of the youth turn toward the church.

1. Undivided attention: A pastor must give his undivided attention to the youth program. This includes his ministry time as well as his personal time.

Oneighty® took Pastor George's undivided attention when he first put his heart into the youth program. Until he put together the model for what is practiced today, Oneighty" took up a lot of his ministry time as well as personal time. Now he does not have to devote the time he initially spent. In the beginning, he went to the teenagers' football games and spoke at morning Bible clubs at their schools. He spent time with the students to learn what they wanted in a youth program. He made the initial investment and is still the driving force behind Oneighty". When I came on board, I did not try to come up with new programs. What is being done today is simply an extension of what initially came out of his heart.

2. Finances and facility: A pastor must designate church finances and provide a facility for the youth.

One night after Oneighty®, a couple of the teenagers invited Pastor George to join them at one of the local pizza places. When he got there, the place was packed with kids who had just left the youth service. A lot of them were crowded around three or four arcade games waiting for a turn.

He thought, *Man, these kids are starving for fellowship. They just want to hang out and have some fun.* We had just spent a lot of money remodeling our youth auditorium, but he decided to make another financial investment in them. He went back and took a good look at the building that housed Oneighty®. At the time, we were also using it for other departments besides the youth ministry. He found different locations for some of these departments and built a game area and a café for the youth group.

Oneighty® began with six or seven arcade games and some pool tables. Within two weeks after opening the expanded facility, Pastor George's initial investment caused an explosion in attendance. Suddenly, Oneighty® was packed out, there were long lines for the arcade games, and we went out and got even more!

3. Influence: A pastor must use his influence on the leaders and the laity.

No one can influence a church better than the pastor can. When Pastor George got involved with the teenagers, it changed the way the entire church viewed the youth ministry. Once people realized he was behind the youth department, they became involved. Additional workers volunteered and resources increased.

Dreams and Visions

Acts 2:17 says, "Your young men shall see visions, and your old men shall dream dreams." The word *young* in this verse literally means "chronological age."[1] The word *old,* however, comes from the word *presbuteros,* which means "older or elder."[2] It speaks of spiritual maturity, someone who is in an "eldership" or leadership position in the church. The words *pastor, bishop,* and *elder* are all derived from this word. This verse says a youthful man will see visions, but a spiritually mature man, or the senior pastor, will dream dreams.

There is a difference between a vision and a dream. The word *vision* refers to a short glimpse into the future. The achievement time of a vision can be measured in terms of months or even years. The word *dream,* on the other hand, indicates an expansive picture of the future. The achievement time of a dream is measured over the course of a lifetime.

I use the analogy of a motion picture to explain the difference of how dreams and visions relate to ministry. God will give the senior pastor a motion picture dream of what he or she has been called to do. Then, He will show the other ministers in the church frames of that dream. Together, they make up a continuous movie that tells the same story. If each frame tells its own story, the movie will be disjointed and hard to understand. When all the frames fit together in proper order, the film makes a dynamic impact on the viewers.

Reflecting Your Pastor's Dream

A youth pastor's first priority should be to follow the dream of the senior pastor. The ministry should reflect his dream. If you are unsure of what the pastor's dream is, you can easily identify it by asking a couple of questions:

- What are the reoccurring themes in his sermons?

- What is his passion in ministry?

- What are the goals of the church?

If your pastor has a passion for praise and worship, you need to reflect that passion in your youth services. Likewise, if missions are a driving force in his ministry, develop a program so the teenagers can also go on mission trips.

Another way to mirror the senior pastor is through your sermons. Your messages to the young people should be in the same vein that your pastor teaches the adults. Although my personal study of the Word may take me in a different direction than what Pastor George is ministering, I still pass on to the teenagers what he is teaching.

They know exactly what his desires and passions are. For example, he places a strong emphasis on soul winning. Therefore, Oneighty® has a dynamic soul-winning program. One of his reoccurring leadership themes is excellence. Therefore, we have made excellence a priority in everything we do.

Some very well-known ministers have spoken at Oneighty®. But without exception, no one receives the kind of reception Pastor George does when he comes to minister. When he is introduced, the kids jump to their feet while cheering and clapping. He has to sit them down because they will not stop. Not only that, but when he is finally able to minister, they listen intently and take notes.

After the meeting is over, none of the workers are goofing around, but they are doing their jobs. He sees excellence in every part of Oneighty®. The kids tell him what they are doing on their school campuses and how they won some of their classmates to the Lord. The entire night he is barraged with a reflection of his heart. He sees the teenagers running with his vision and cannot do enough to help.

Developing Your Pastor's Trust and Support

After you have identified your pastor's dream, there are four keys to complementing it and thereby gaining his trust. Once his trust is gained, he will become your biggest fan and his support will automatically follow.

1. Adapt to your pastor's leadership style.

Everyone leads and manages differently. You can go to any bookstore and find hundreds of books on management. It is amazing that each author has a testimony about how he or she successfully manages his or her company. Each management style, however, uses different methods for success. Each type of leadership or management style is unique to the situation.

Every pastor has a different style of leadership. Although your pastor's style may vary from your own, it is important that your style flow with his. You are not in charge. He is the leader, and you are the follower. Your responsibility is to flow with the structure and management style of his leadership.

One of my former interns had worked as a youth pastor for approximately six months when I received a call from him. He was frustrated because he was not able to flow with his pastor's style of management. He liked structure and would work at the church from eight to five every day. His pastor, however, might arrive at eleven, twelve, or even one o'clock. Sometimes, he would not come in at all. He liked to spend time early in the morning in prayer. He also felt he was more productive when he worked from home. The youth pastor did not like that. He wanted to be able to drop by the pastor's office to ask questions or receive advice. The pastor was usually unavailable when the youth pastor needed him.

When I asked my young charge about the church, he said it was exploding. Although they were new, they were running over a thousand people. The youth group, on the other hand, was not doing well at all. There were only thirty or forty kids attending his services.

He asked me what to do. I said, "Maybe you need to stay home in the mornings!" My point to him was to adapt to his pastor's style. His youth group was not growing because it did not reflect the pastor's heart or vision for the church. He was actually fighting his pastor totally unaware. Instead of putting his pastor down, he needed to learn some things from him. The lesson to learn is to adapt to the leadership style of your pastor. If you will work in submission to him, you will discover his style will work for you as well.

2.   Learn how to communicate effectively.

Good communication begins with a respect for your pastor's time. I have never seen a pastor who had a lot of free time—whether he has a congregation of fifty, five hundred, or five thousand. Ineffective forms of communication include stopping him in the hall before he heads out the door. After a church service is never a good time to speak with him. Whatever you do, don't barge into his office and say you need a half-hour of his time!

I have found one of the best ways to communicate is through memos that include action lines: Approved; Not approved; Approved with the following revisions. Pastor George can read the memo whenever he has time, make his comments, and shoot it back to me. It is quite effective, and I have not wasted any of his time.

3. Prepare adequately for your meetings.

When you need a meeting with your pastor, provide an agenda before your appointment. This will let him know what you want to discuss so he can mentally prepare for the meeting.

Then, come prepared. Bring solutions to problems and several options when a decision is required. Let's say, for instance, you are planning an outreach and need to purchase some mobile sound equipment. Rather than saying, "Pastor, we need some sound equipment for an event we would like to hold. What do you think we should get?" Go to the meeting with all the details outlined, such as the location, the date(s), and how many kids you expect to attend.

Give him options to make a decision. For instance, tell him why you need the sound equipment and the consequences if you do not have it. Research the purchase thoroughly. What would it cost to buy? What would it cost to rent? What, if any, are the advantages of buying versus renting? Obtain quotes from at least three different vendors. If you come to the meeting prepared, your pastor will be able to respond quickly.

4. Keep your pastor's visibility high in the youth ministry.

It would be a sad commentary for your teenagers to graduate from the youth program and not know their pastor! Oneighty® works hard to keep Pastor George's visibility high in our youth program. There are many ways to achieve this. There is a photo of Pastor George hanging in the lobby next to the vision of Oneighty®. I also refer to him frequently in my messages. He speaks at Oneighty® regularly, often once a month. Although he is no longer deeply involved in the day-to-day activities of the youth ministry, he continues to set the agenda and attend football games, and our young people know he believes in them.

Developing the Blueprints of Youth Ministry

Once you are committed to your pastor's dream, you can develop the blueprint of your youth ministry. Begin by defining your vision in a written statement.

Jesus had a mission statement for His ministry. It is found in Luke 4:18-19.

> The Spirit of the Lord is upon me, because he hath anointed me to preach the gospel to the poor; he hath sent me to heal the brokenhearted, to preach deliverance to the captives, and recovering of sight to the blind, to set at liberty them that are bruised, to preach the acceptable year of the Lord.

From this statement, we see that Jesus knew His purpose in life and clearly defined how He intended to fulfill His destiny. At the beginning of His ministry, He released His vision through a blueprint. He said, "This is what I am here to do, this is where I am going, and this is how I will accomplish my vision." I believe it is important for you to do the same thing in your ministry as well. You need to establish a set of goals so people can climb on board and become excited about where you are going. Next, develop a clear plan to fulfill the vision God gave you. Those who are helping you, your staff and volunteers, should also be aware of your plan.

I see much of what I call "Charlie Brown" youth ministry. A cartoon I saw years ago inspired this name. In the first illustration, Charlie Brown had a bow and arrow and was getting ready to shoot the arrow. In the next picture, he and Lucy were watching the arrow fly through the air. In the last illustration, they were standing next to the arrow and Charlie Brown was painting a red bull's eye around the arrow!

Much of youth ministry is like that today. Youth pastors blindly shoot arrows in the air hoping to hit something—anything. Then they assume that whatever they hit was what the Lord intended for them to do. They end up painting a bull's eye around anything. We need to be proactive in ministry and first obtain direction from the Lord on what steps to take. You have to know what you are shooting at before you know if you hit your target. Only then can you plan steps to accomplish your vision.

The Power of Vision

In 1971 a Disney executive, along with one of his engineers, was admiring the newly completed Disney World project in Orlando, Florida. Construction alone on the monumental theme park and resort had taken over four years to complete. While viewing their accomplishments, the engineer sadly shook his head and said, "Man, if Walt

Disney could have only seen this!" He had died of lung cancer five years earlier. The elder executive looked at the young man and said, "He did. That is why it's here!"

Vision is so powerful that it will outlast its creator. Once you learn how to develop and articulate your vision, other people will pick it up and run with it. Even if God moves you into another area of ministry, the vision will continue to spread as your workers take the reins of the ministry.

Working without a vision is like straightening chairs on the Titanic. You can try to put the chairs where they need to be, but it is useless action if the ship is sinking. All your serving and sweating will not help keep the ship afloat unless you have a vision and know where you are headed. Your ministry will float aimlessly until one day when you run into something that will sink the whole thing.

The Oneighty® Vision

The mission statement of Oneighty® is "Jesus Christ and His plans for teenagers." Our mission is to compel thousands to follow Christ, to be equipped with His Word, and to proclaim His message. Our vision statement is more specific in that it outlines how we plan to accomplish our mission. The three parts of the vision are:

1. We see a method of reaching teenagers who love God but don't like church.

According to studies done by George Barna, President of Barna Research Group Ltd., a marketing research firm located in Ventura, California, 95 percent of all high school students believe in God.[3] If you ask them if they believe in Jesus, they will tell you yes. However, when you ask them if they go to church, you will find they do not attend church and don't like it. According to the World Christian Encyclopedia, 53,000 people leave church every week never to return.[4] Teenagers make up a good portion of those numbers.

At Oneighty®, we do not have to try to get teenagers to believe there is a God. We are not dealing with an atheistic culture. They do not have a problem with God or Jesus. They feel God is cool and what Jesus did was cool, but church—forget it! They are really saying they do not like you or what you represent. They do not like church buildings or the way we worship. Our biggest job is to change the stereotypical images lodged in their minds about church.

Usually their childhood memories of church include wearing stiff, starchy clothes that squeaked when they walked. They wore dress shoes that either hurt their feet or caused them to slip and slide. They sang hymn after hymn and then sat in uncomfortable chairs listening to dry, boring preachers talk about something they could not relate to. Consequently, their perception of church is terrible. We are fighting a losing battle unless we find a way to eradicate the stereotypes that hold the youth at bay from our churches and youth groups.

2. We see a mandate to equip teenagers to win life's battles with raised shields and drawn swords.

We are teaching young people the Word of God. We want them to learn how to stand on their own two feet spiritually and walk in victory. It is our desire that they learn how to live for God and have a personal relationship with Him. Our goal is to teach them how to stand in faith and speak the Word. In times of trials, we want them to know God will help them and answer their prayers.

3. We see a movement of teenagers who will not sit back and watch their world go to hell.

Finally, in fulfilling the third part of our vision, we want to develop soul winners and mobilize teenagers for evangelism in their world. We want to see a movement of teenagers who will take on an evangelistic heart and will not sit back and watch their world go to hell.

Imparting Vision

Proverbs 29:18 NIV says, "Where there is no revelation [or vision], the people cast off restraint." The phrase "cast off restraint" means people—or in this case the young people—would become undisciplined and uncommitted. Teenagers become apathetic in their life because they do not have a vision. Parents come to me all the time because their children are bored with church and Christianity. My advice to them is to give their children a vision for their life and future. Get them involved in serving in church, not just playing the role of a spectator!

My wife and I work with our three boys to develop vision for their lives. We ask them, "Where is God leading you? What gifts and talents has He placed in your life?" We get them to make short-term and long-term goals. A short-term goal might be as simple as becoming one of the best basketball players on their team. A long-term goal helps steer the course of their life.

One of my sons loves the performing arts. He enjoys acting and wants to someday direct movies. I am helping him develop his vision. One time when I was scheduled to minister in California, I asked him to come with me so we could tour movie studios. We were even able to take a private tour of Steven Speilberg's Dreamworks studio. That trip made a big impression on him and gave him a vision for his future. I promise you, he will never allow anything to shipwreck his vision. He has a passion and a desire he wants to see fulfilled in his life.

The same thing will happen in your youth program as teenagers get a vision for the youth ministry. They will see they have ownership in the program and have a part to play in its success. Each of your students has different gifts. As their talents are funneled into various ministries, their vision for the youth ministry will develop. They will see how they have a major part in making the vision happen. We have seen that as kids find their place in Oneighty®, they are no longer lethargic. They are excited because they have a vision for their future.

The Oneighty® Acrostic

We have developed a simple way to teach our students and leaders our vision by making an acrostic out of the word *Oneighty.*

> **"O" is for Outreach.** We are outreach-minded and teach the importance of winning souls. We teach our students how to go out and win their classmates, their family, and anyone they meet to the Lord.

> **"N" is for Numerical Increase.** God wants us to grow in numbers. We are not comparing ourselves with another church but working to keep large numbers of young people from going to hell. The more numbers we reach, the less numbers the kingdom of darkness has.

> **"E" is for Exalting Christ.** We exalt Jesus—in our worship, in our lifestyle, and in everything we do.

> **"I" is for Involving Students.** We want to see young people involved in serving. We need the help of adults, but we are not an adult-based youth group. Our students are plugged into every area of ministry.

"G" is for Growing Spiritually. We want to see our young people have a deeper relationship with Christ and become spiritually mature through discipleship.

"H" is for Having Fun. We incorporate fun into everything we do. If we go on a two-week mission trip, two of those days are set aside for fun things. God wants us to enjoy our environment, our relationships, and, most of all, life itself.

"T" is for Training Leaders. We are committed to training leaders, both students and adults, to be thoroughly equipped to minister to the needs of teens.

"Y" is for Youth Friendly Facilities. We have created an environment that is appealing to both the churched and unchurched teenagers.

Inspiring Vision in Those Who Follow

The vision of the leader must always be a little larger than the vision of the followers. It is your responsibility to lead and guide your workers through each step of what God has called you to do.

The book *Built to Last* by James C. Collins and Jerry I. Porras documents the Fortune 500 companies that have been in business the longest during the past hundred years.[5] Many of these companies come and go. In fact, over the last ten years, less than half of the businesses that made it to the Fortune 500 list are still there today.

There is one common trait among the companies that have remained on the list for decades. They all have BHAGs. That stands for "Big Hairy Audacious Goals"! The research of Collins and Porras shows the companies that continue to grow are the ones that never relax their vision, but set bigger and bigger goals. They never allow themselves to become complacent, but are continually striving for the next level.

When a company has limited goals, they typically begin to relax and coast when their goals are reached. Once they start to coast, the business begins a downward descent. Before long, it has vanished.

As a leader, you are the goal setter to take your ministry to the next level. Although you know the big picture, you have to set realistic steps for your followers. If you tell them everything at once, you will scare off many people.

For example, if you have only ten kids in your youth program, do not tell them your vision is for fifty thousand teenagers to attend. Give them a realistic goal by starting with plans to reach fifty students. As you attain your goals, expand your vision to seventy-five, then one hundred, and so on. That way you are always stretching people without overwhelming them.

TOUGH QUESTIONS

Q: What do I do if my pastor doesn't support our youth ministry?

A: First, you're not alone. Do not feel discouraged. There have been many youth pastors who have felt like that. I think the key is not to get bitter or upset, or isolate yourself and become mad at your pastor. Understand that your pastor is very busy, he has many things going on, and pastors can only do so many things at once. I'd begin by praying for your pastor. Pray that God will encourage him and open his eyes to the importance of reaching the next generation, and that he'll catch the heart of reaching kids. Then, be the biggest supporter of your pastor. If you want to reap support, you have to give it. Be faithful, be loyal, cheer him on, encourage him, and let him know how much you appreciate him. If you give that kind of support, you'll receive it. From time to time put materials in his hands, whether it's a good tape or video on youth ministry, or different books that might encourage and inspire him along the way—maybe the story of a ministry like Oneighty" so he can see a pastor like mine, who has made a commitment to youth ministry and seen incredible results in both the youth group and the growth of our church. I think if you do those things, prayer support, encouragement, and materials, you will see his heart turn.

Q: Honestly Blaine, I don't even have a vision for our youth ministry. What do I do?

A: Well, that is a tough question. Begin by going to the Lord in prayer. There have been times when, I have to admit, I've been so discouraged in youth ministry that I wondered if I still had a vision for it anymore. In those times, I found myself going back to God, praying and saying, **Lord, help me, speak to my heart, show me what to do.** It is amazing how the Lord can give you vision, compassion, and the desire to reach kids, and then beyond that, give you a strategy and the steps to take to get there. If after praying and sincerely seeking God you still don't feel like you have a vision and a calling to reach young people, go talk to your pastor. Share your heart and see if there is another place for you in the church. Maybe there is someone else who feels a deep sense of calling and burden for the kids of your church.

Q: I have more vision than I have time. How can I possibly get it all done?

A: Well, join the crowd. We all have more vision than we have time. I have been in full-time youth ministry for 20 years, but even today, I've put a lot of time into this. I have eleven staff members and ten interns, all full-time, and we still don't have enough time to do all the vision we have. You will never have enough time. The key is to prioritize and find what is most important right now in your ministry, what you absolutely need to be doing, and do those things. Do those things well, and be willing to say you cannot do everything. Constantly train new leaders and new people you can delegate to. Every time you delegate to someone, you are multiplying your time in someone else and helping him or her fulfill his or her part of the body of Christ. Continue to raise more people so you can expand your vision and create more time to do other things.

rule two:

IF YOUR VISION IS FROM GOD, IT WILL COME TO PASS

How many times have you heard that if something is from God, it will happen? However, just because a vision is from God does not mean it will come to pass. The failure to realize a dream does not lie with God but rather with people. Too often people incorrectly think that what God has spoken to their hearts will automatically manifest. When it doesn't, they either think they missed God, or, not wanting to admit that, say, "Oh, God really wanted me to do such and such." They never took the time to develop a strategy to bring about the vision, and therefore, the dream was never realized.

Rule Two: *If your vision is from God, it will come to pass.*

Many ministers and lay people have become discouraged and left when they believed this rule but did not see their vision manifest. The truth that needs to replace it deals with the implementation of the vision.

Truth Two: *Vision is achieved by strategic action and aggressive vision.*

Proverbs 21:31 AMP says, "The horse is prepared for the day of battle, but deliverance and victory are of the Lord." This Scripture tells us to prepare our horse before the day of battle. We train the animal for war, properly feed it, and outfit it with battle gear. Once we have done our part, God promises to give us victory. We both have work to do.

God is into strategy. Before He created Adam and Eve, He knew they were going to sin against Him. He had already come up with a plan to turn things around. Likewise, when He gives us a vision, He wants us to take the time to plan our course. He will then direct our path with well-defined steps. (Prov. 16:9.)

The "Seven Days of Creation" Process

At Oneighty®, whenever we decide to host a new event or develop a new outreach, we always put our ideas through a process that we call the "Seven Days of Creation."

We never eliminate any of the steps. If you do, the vision can be aborted. The book of Proverbs refers to people who put much thought into what they are doing as intelligent. It says, "An intelligent mind acquires knowledge" (Prov. 18:15 RSV).

Day One: Brainstorm

Plan a session with at least three other people to pray, think, and dream creatively. This is a time to do "visionary" brainstorming. By visionary, I mean thinking beyond what you or other ministries are already doing. You want to come up with fresh ideas. Begin by coming up with what may appear to be wild and outlandish suggestions. Then polish the best idea into something that can work.

Keys to Effective Brainstorming

1. Invite creative, passionate people.

People filled with passion and creativity believe anything can change, regardless of the situation. Pessimists, on the other hand, will find reasons to shoot down any new idea. They do not like change and do not believe anything good can come out of brainstorming. You don't want people with this type of attitude involved. They will only hinder your planning session.

You might have heard the story about the two young boys who were left in a room full of manure. One was a pessimist, the other an optimist. The pessimistic youngster sat in a corner crying because he was left in such a filthy place. The optimist, however, was having a great time chucking horse manure everywhere. The crying lad said, "What are you doing?" He exclaimed, "With all this stuff, there has to be a pony in here somewhere!"

You want this type of person in your brainstorming sessions. It does not matter what kind of "stuff" is lying around, he or she believes something can be done. This person can always come up with a way to improve the situation.

2. Brainstorming is "storming."

Brainstorming is not a light wind; it is a storm. Anything goes. The intention is to throw out anything and everything. As ideas come, write everything down. A bad idea might lead to a good one. You never know which suggestion will lead to the idea that will help you come up with the solution to what you need to do. This is not the time to analyze the ideas. That will come later.

3. Choose one area at a time to brainstorm.

You cannot brainstorm your entire ministry in one session. You will be pulled in too many directions and will not be able to effectively impact any one department. Instead, look at each department or proposal separately.

For example, examine your youth service. How you can attract more unchurched kids? Are you keeping the attention of the youth during the service? If not, where do you lose them? How can you change this?

After you are finished with one area of ministry, move on to another department. Eventually, every area will be covered.

4. Invite teenagers.

They know what they like. They are who you are trying to reach anyway. When we met to brainstorm the development of an invitation for the teenagers to pass out at their schools, we included both adults and teenagers. We found that what the adults thought were great ideas, the kids thought were bad.

Your teenagers are the ones who will read your materials. You also want them to share your products with their friends. If the design is outdated, they will never pick it up, let alone pass it along to someone else. When we finished brainstorming our invitation, we came up with a cool-looking piece our young people wanted to hand out.

Day Two: Brainwork

Most people do not like this step. Brainwork includes a lot of research. This is where you take the good ideas and determine if they are feasible. Everything is examined—from costs to manpower, time, facilities, and finally promotion of the event, outreach, or product. Don't leave any stone unturned. You don't want to assume that an idea can or cannot be done; you have to make sure it is feasible. The more work you do on the front end, the more surprises you will avoid as you start to put the idea into operation.

As you research and realize that what you want to do will be costly, don't throw out a good idea because of expense alone. Although something may cost more money than you have budgeted, continue in the development of the idea and allow God to move on your behalf.

We wanted our Oneighty® invitation to look sharp, which meant printing in four-colors. That would cost a lot of money, and during the process, we thought it might be necessary to cut the project back to one or two colors. Then we reconsidered, "Let's just see what it will cost."

We shared with a printer our vision of inviting every high school student in Tulsa to Oneighty®. He became excited and wanted to be part of what we were doing. When we discussed the printing cost, he said he would donate the first print run and run the second printing at a discounted price!

We printed ten thousand invitations, thinking they would last awhile. Our teenagers liked them so much they handed out all the invitations in just three months, which meant going back for a second printing much sooner than we had anticipated!

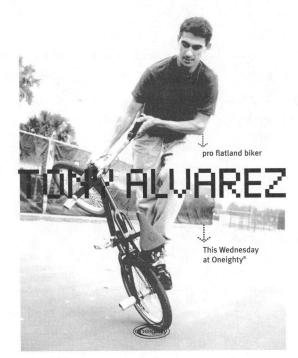

pro flatland biker

TONY ALVAREZ

This Wednesday
at Oneighty®

DO YOU LIKE TO WHEELIE?

If you think the wheelie is cool—and we all do—your gonna love this week at Oneighty®. We're bringing in Tony Alvarez, pro flatland biking champion. Tony has performed in front of an estimated 15 million people. Come and be amazed. We're also bringing in one of the largest outdoor climbing walls you have ever fallen off of and a horse load of free food for an evening that will blow your mind and kick start your heart.

More info? Need a ride?
Call Oneighty® at 234-8180.

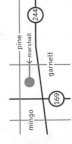

Day Three: Paper Transfer

When God spoke to the prophet Habakkuk, He said, "Write the vision, and make it plain upon tables, that he may run that readeth it" (Hab. 2:2). Every part of your vision has to be transferred to paper in some form so people can see it. Paper transfer will take on different forms depending on what you are doing.

For instance, if you are planning a community outreach with guest speakers, guest musicians, and many activities, the paper transfer of the vision for that event will take the form of a postcard, brochure, or flyer.

In another area of your ministry, God may have provided a plan on how to structure your campus ministry and effectively train your student and adult leaders. The paper transfer will be in the form of a training manual, which should include an outline of your plan of action for reaching the high school campuses you want to target. All the information workers need to know about ministry protocol will be written down. As you bring your teams in for training, everyone will understand exactly what they are supposed to do and how you want them to minister in schools.

JOB DESCRIPTION

Title: **Oneighty® Greeter Director**
Department: COTM Oneighty® Senior High Youth

1. Be prayed-up before you arrive at Oneighty®.
   - Pray for Pastor/speaker
   - That the hearts of the youth will be open
   - That everything will run decently and in order
   - That God will use you as an example to the youth of Oneighty®.

2. Be at Oneighty® 45 minutes before service starts.

3. Go to Greeter Room.
   - Post applicable signs on doors.
   - Make sure you have bulletins for that week.
   - Give greeter assignment.

4. When greeters arrive 30 minutes before service, give them their assignments for the night.

5. Pray as a team for the speaker, service, teens.

6. Supervise your greeters while they are greeting.

7. Greeters are to remain at doors until service begins.
   - You will need to keep one set of greeters at the doors for 5 minutes after service starts, for late comers!

8. Make sure that you are outgoing, friendly, and try to remember as many of the teens' names as possible and use them!

9. Personal Hygiene
   - Be sure to have clean hands, fresh breath, and a bright smile.

10. Dress - GIVE GOD YOUR VERY BEST!
    - Men: Acceptable: Pants, Oneighty® Staff Shirt (18 years +), Tennis shoes Unacceptable: shorts, cut-off shirts, sandals without socks
    - Women: Acceptable: Pants, skirt, Oneighty® Staff Shirt (18 years +) Unacceptable: shorts, mini-skirts, sandals without socks

11. You are responsible to make a schedule for your workers each month. It should be printed and mailed or distributed to your workers 1-2 weeks in advance.

Paper transfer will also take the form of job descriptions. Every position in each of your departments needs to have one. For example, when students want to become a greeter, they will know what is required of them and how you expect them to accomplish their assignment. Training is another part of paper transfer. It becomes much easier for the trainer and trainee when procedures are already written down.

Day Four: Champion the Cause

You have to constantly promote your vision to others. Whether it is over lunch with one person, to your entire youth group, or in front of the adult church, you have to champion your cause. As you talk about what you are doing and where you are going, you will motivate others to come on board and help bring your vision to pass. If you do not do this, you will not be able to attain the support you need to accomplish what God has spoken to your heart.

Day Five: Draft

There is a difference between presenting a need and presenting an opportunity to serve. You probably will not get many volunteers by presenting needs. But when you share your vision and give people the opportunity to be a part of it, you will see a dramatic increase in the number of people you are able to recruit.

With the completion of "Day Two, Brainwork," you will be able to present a systematic strategy to accomplish your goals. As people listen, they will see where they can fit in. One person may not be able to help with step one but will want to play a role in step three. On the other hand, they might know of someone who can assist you in one aspect of the plan. In the end, all pieces of the puzzle will find their right place and everyone will be able to see the completed vision.

After new recruits have signed up to help, follow-up needs to begin within the first week. If you do not do this, you will lose some of your new people. It is not that they do not want to help, but other things can crop up in their life that will pull them away from their opportunity to serve. With immediate follow-up and training, you can plug them in right away and that will give legs to your vision.

Day Six: Instruct

After you have drafted your team, the next step is to instruct or equip them with the skills and knowledge they need to succeed. We have training sessions for all departments. When someone begins to work with us, we never assume he or she will figure out what to do. We thoroughly train our staff and volunteers. We provide instruction on how we want things to be done. There is no question about what they are supposed to do.

When we distributed the Oneighty® invitation, we used drama to train the teens how to invite friends to the youth ministry. We wrote a skit about a student passing out the invitation to his classmates and showed some of the reactions he might encounter. When our young people took the invitation to pass out in real life, they were not thrown off guard by the responses of their fellow classmates.

Day Seven: Do Game Films

This means to evaluate and continually improve your performance. Just because a plan does not come off perfectly does not mean you should quit. Go back to the drawing board and improve your skills. Look at what you did right and what you did wrong. Come up with a list of areas that need improvement. What can be done to make sure a mistake is not repeated? If everything went smoothly, how can you make it even better next time?

We have improved upon every original idea we had for all our ministries at Oneighty®. After a project is completed, we examine it again six months to a year later. We analyze and strategize until we come up with ideas that will take us to the next level.

By constantly looking for areas of improvement, you will never become stagnant but continue to evolve. Your continual growth and improvement will cause your workers to grow and improve as they work alongside you.

As you study and implement the process of "Seven Days of Creation," you will begin to see the vision for each area of your youth ministry come to pass. As I look back over the years and analyze the visions I have had but did not happen in my life, I have come to realize that I skipped some of the steps in this process. I guarantee if your vision is truly from God and you perform all seven steps, your vision will be fulfilled.

TOUGH QUESTIONS

Q: When we brainstorm, one of our leaders seems to quench the enthusiasm with constant criticism of ideas. How do I handle this?

A: After one session, if you see that happening, very quickly meet with that person privately and explain. They may not even know they're doing it. They may have a habit of doing it, and you certainly don't want that in a brainstorming session.

You want to create optimism, excitement, and a "can do" attitude. Meet with them, give them examples of how they've quenched the spirit of creativity in your session, and ask them not to do it anymore.

Just say, "Listen, I can't have this, and if it continues in future meetings or brainstorming sessions, I'm going to have to exclude you and I don't want to do that, but I will have to." Then you must follow through on that.

I've had to do it. I've had leaders, and even staff members, who did not flow with the team. They did not encourage, were not creative, and were constantly bringing other volunteers, leaders, and staff members down. After a meeting once or twice, I had to ask them to step away from our creative team. It is a tough decision, but it's important to do in order to keep people excited, motivated, and moving forward.

Q: I'm not a very good planner. What can I do to improve in this area?

A: Force yourself to plan. Sit down with your key team members. That does not include all your workers, but only the key players on your team. Open the calendar and plan together.

Make yourself plan, talk about what you are going to do this spring in the summer, and discuss how you can launch the fall campaign with the schools. Write things down, put things on the calendar, and then begin to decide how to go from there. How do you get organized to make this happen?

Learn from those who are good planners. Open your eyes, and when you see people who are planners with their day-timers and every hour of the day accounted for, ask questions." How do you do that? Why do you do that? Learn from those who are good planners.

Q: We went through the seven steps to develop a new ministry outreach and it failed. What now?

A: First, realize we have all failed. I have gone through the seven steps on projects or events we have done, and they have not always worked. Sometimes the question is, Did the Lord tell you to do it? Reevaluate that.

Second, maybe the Lord told you to do it, but you didn't do it at the right time. Timing can be the issue, and you didn't hit the timing exactly right. You have to go back to the drawing board, evaluate, and ask questions. Ask yourself how you can do it right the next time. Do you need to throw this out and say it was not a good plan for you?

The main thing is not to quit. Do not give up just because something didn't work, because we have all been there.

rule three:

Become a close friend and confidant to all your teenagers

When I started in youth ministry, I believed that to be successful you had to become a close friend to all the teenagers in your youth group. I felt if I did not become their confidant, I would not be able to influence their lives, and ultimately, the outreach would not grow.

I do not know how the third time-honored rule got started. It is one of the worst rules that a youth pastor could embrace.

Rule Three: *Become a close friend and confidant to all your teenagers.*

When this rule is followed, instead of aiding, you are actually stunting the growth of your ministry. Ultimately, you will not be able to reach your community. It is impossible to become a friend and confidant of every young person who comes to your youth group. If you try, you will limit your outreach to about thirty or forty kids. This is approximately the maximum number of teenagers a youth pastor can have a personal relationship with at one time. If you attempt to have a meaningful relationship with more than that, you will find yourself stretched too thin to be an effective leader.

How can you have a personal touch among your young people if you are not personally involved in their lives? You want them to feel loved and accepted when they come to your meetings.

To address this need, we have replaced the third rule with the following truth, which develops a leadership structure that enables the young people to have personal contact with someone other than the youth pastor.

Truth Three: *Unselfish youth pastors learn how to release a cascade of leadership in their youth ministry.*

You can reach more young people through a combined effort. If you develop your leadership, you are able to reach more students in your community than you could ever accomplish by yourself. Properly trained leaders can make the same impact in the lives of young people as you can.

Right now our Wednesday night service averages fourteen hundred to sixteen hundred kids. It would be impossible to even try to have a personal relationship with that many people. They have embraced me as their youth pastor, but there are a number of trained leaders in every area of our ministry who can reach them one-on-one. Consequently, they do not feel neglected but rather a part of the ministry.

Kids are not disappointed when they leave Oneighty® because they did not meet me. They leave saying, "Man, I had a great time!" It is not about me. It is about ministry and what God is doing. I do not want you to think I never spend any time with the kids. I am very accessible to my youth group. However, a young person who needs to talk or request prayer does not have to come to me. Other people are available to help them.

I encourage you to decentralize your leadership. You do not have to touch everything, and you cannot do all the work by yourself.

Biblical Leadership Structure

The development of leadership structure in ministry is a scriptural principle found throughout the Bible. We see it in the life of Moses. After he brought the children of Israel out of Egypt, he tried to govern the entire population by himself. His father-in-law saw what he was doing and advised him to raise up leaders and appoint them over smaller groups to serve as judges over the people. They would handle simple disputes, while the difficult cases would be brought to Moses. This lightened Moses' load because many would share it. (Ex. 18:13-26.)

In Matthew 10, Jesus multiplied His effectiveness by sending His disciples out to heal the sick, cast out devils, and raise the dead. Until that point He had been the only one who ministered to the people. Jesus instructed the disciples to minister in His power and ability, and they were able to reach more people together.

Jesus always involved His disciples. While He was with them, He demonstrated that He did not have to be the only miracle-worker. He taught them how to minister to others by laying hands on the sick and casting out devils. He duplicated Himself in each of their lives by training them how to minister.

He established a model that could be followed throughout the ages during His short, three-year ministry on the earth. He not only left us a handbook, the Bible, He also gave us the Holy Spirit to lead and guide us through the process. Now it is up to us to use these tools and touch lives.

Franchising Your Ministry

Do you want your youth ministry to be a "mom and pop" operation that serves the same customers every week? There are not too many "mom and pop" stores around anymore. The reason is they never tried to expand. They were happy as long as a few customers came by every week. It was enough to pay the bills. Most, if not all, of these shops are out of business today because of retailers like Wal-Mart, who have a vision to sell their products to every consumer across America.

Consider the franchise approach for your ministry. This may be a new concept for you, but consider franchising not only yourself but also the things God has put inside you. Franchising is simply replicating what you are doing through your trained workers. You are authorizing them to duplicate your vision.

Most people have probably not heard of Ray Kroc; however, there is no one in the United States today who is not familiar with his product. He is the man behind McDonald's and the creative force for the concept of franchising. His first restaurant opened in 1955, and through franchising, or duplicating the original restaurant, the McDonald's Corporation currently has restaurants in 120 countries around the world.

The Leadership Cascade

The same principle of franchising can be transferred to ministry in what I call the Leadership Cascade. The apostle Paul speaks of it in 2 Timothy 2:2: "And the things that thou hast heard of me among many witnesses, the same commit thou to faithful men, who shall be able to teach others also."

Paul first learned from Jesus and then taught Timothy, his young protégé. Timothy was also instructed to teach faithful men who would teach others.

II Timothy 2:2 And the things that thou hast heard of me among many witnesses, the same commit thou to faithful men, who shall be able to teach others also.

This model is an example for us to follow today. The head of the church, the Lord Jesus Christ, speaks to the senior pastor. He or she in turn speaks to the youth pastor. Leadership does not stop with the youth pastor. Paul specifically told Timothy to entrust to faithful men what he had learned. The youth pastor, therefore, entrusts to his or her core leadership group what the senior pastor has passed on to him or her. Once your leadership core embraces the vision that has been passed down to them, they in turn will reach others.

There are several key words found in the leadership cascade. The first is **entrust.** It means to give to another for care, protection, and performance and implies importance. You do not "hand off" to others what you value as precious. You **entrust** it to them. Timothy regarded the truths Paul taught him with great importance. He treated what he had learned as something precious. The way you instill the preciousness of your vision to your leaders is by working closely with them.

The next key word is **faithful.** Often we associate faithfulness with consistency or always being on time. Faithful people are those who can be counted on to be there when you need them. Another common definition is those who do what they say they are going to do. These definitions are only part of faithfulness.

The way I define faithfulness is being true to the original in vision, doctrine, and spirit. As youth pastor, the young people look to you for leadership. You are spearheading the senior pastor's vision for youth ministry. Likewise, you want your core group of leaders to be true to the vision.

I can have leaders who are always on time in their department and in place but are unfaithful by taking their department in a different direction than the vision of Oneighty®. If their vision for the department is different than mine, they are unfaithful. They can also be unfaithful in doctrine. They might believe and teach a doctrine we do not believe. A leader might not agree with the way we do our outreach to students. Instead of submitting, they try to lead them in a different direction. When a leader is not true to your vision, he or she only brings division to the ministry.

The final key word is the phrase **who will be able.** This phrase refers to ability and indicates a need for training. Typically, in the secular world, as well as in the church, people put ability first. According to this Scripture, ability is the last part of the cascade structure.

As you recruit leaders, look for faithful people. These people will be true to your vision, doctrine, and spirit. Then, spend time entrusting your vision to them. Finally, train them so they are able to carry out the mission.

Delegation Without Definition Brings Disaster

The art of delegation will buy you time and give others joy. However, delegating by the seat of your pants will waste your time and bring shame to others. You cannot be sloppy in delegating. By that I mean, you cannot see someone and say, "Hey, do the audio," or, "Hey, we need you to do drama."

What may appear to be the easy way out of delegation is to tell a person the results of what you want and let them figure out how to do it. Every time I have delegated something that way, I have only become frustrated. I did not get the results I wanted and ended up doing the assignment myself. However, that person was not to blame—I was. I did not delegate the task properly.

When you delegate, you have to give a clear definition of what you are asking a person to do. You have to show him what you want done and how you want it done. A principle I follow closely is this: Only do tomorrow what you have time to train for today. I do not plan anything in ministry that I have not first trained my workers to do. I never delegate to someone who is unfaithful.

Here is a good example of proper delegation. I wanted a drama team for Oneighty®. In fact, the set on the stage was built, but it just sat there. It looked good, but nothing ever happened on it. There wasn't a leader who could direct the drama department, and I didn't have time to assemble a skit every week.

Finally, a young woman who had been faithfully serving at Oneighty® came to me. She had experience in the performing arts and wanted to help. Before I entrusted her with the drama department, I sat down and outlined my vision. I wanted comical skits to act as icebreakers in the service. They should last no longer than five minutes and set the stage for the message. The skit would set the stage for a certain subject, and the message would provide the answers.

In the beginning we wrote the skits together, along with the help of a couple of staff members. Then I explained how the rehearsal schedule should go. Initially, I attended the first couple of rehearsals and worked with the actors. When I released the department to her, I felt confident she could handle the task. More importantly, I knew she would be faithful to the Oneighty® vision.

Ministries should be modeled before you release them to workers. This should be done with each department. Some areas of ministry will be relatively simple, requiring only a couple of hours to model. Others may take a few weeks. It is important to take the time to show your leaders what you want and then train them before you turn them loose.

The great thing about developing leaders is your presence can be multiplied. One time I had agreed to be interviewed on TV in Tulsa, as well as speak at a worker training session at Dry Gulch USA, our 470-acre ministry camp. I had forgotten to put the training session on my calendar. When I agreed to do the TV interview, I did not realize I had committed to another engagement for the same time. I needed to be in two places about fifty miles apart and could not change either appointment.

The solution was simple. I delegated the training session to one of my associate pastors. He had worked with me since he was nineteen years old. A lot of time and knowledge had been invested in him. I knew he was capable of teaching the session. After the interview, I returned to the church just as the workers were arriving from the training session at the camp. They were excited about what they had learned. They even told me my associate's teaching was just as good, if not better, than mine was!

The wonderful thing about developing a leadership cascade is that you can multiply yourself and what God has put inside of you for others to enjoy. Your ministry can operate without you always being present because you know your leaders will share your heart.

Becoming a Better Leader

The leadership cascade is only as good as your own personal leadership and character. You want to make sure what you are passing on to them is filled with integrity. If you will examine yourself in the five following ways, your leadership will have an impact in the lives of those you are developing.

1. Lead by influence not position.

Only 7 percent of communication are through words.[1] The remaining 93 percent rests on the influence we have with other people. I am talking about your credibility. How you conduct your life has an impact on the words you say. I do not want you to feel that words are not important because they are, but the lifestyle you lead away from church is critical as a youth pastor.

What kind of ministry will you have if you stand before your youth leaders and say, "God has spoken to me, and we are going to do such and such," then after church you are spotted renting an X-rated movie at the video store? How will your words influence your staff and students? The next time you get up to preach, they will look at you and think, **What a hypocrite!** Words are important, but they will not have any impact if your actions cause you to lose your influence in the lives of your young people.

I usually play hockey every Monday night. When the game is over, we sit around and talk about how we can improve the game. Over the years I have noticed that it does not matter who has the "C" on his jersey. "C" stands for captain. He is usually the person who talks to the referee if there are disputes on the ice. The team, however, does not necessarily look to the captain for advice. They will look to the individual who has the most influence among them. It does not matter if he is the captain or not.

I encourage you to strive to be a person of influence with your youth ministry. Let your lifestyle affect the lives of those you lead for the better.

2. You attract and reproduce what you are, so become a good prototype.

Your leadership team is a mirror of your character and ability. If you are unorganized, your staff will be unorganized. If you highly esteem work ethics and moral standards, so will your staff. If you do not like what you see in your ministry, first examine your own life and how you are leading.

People like to follow men and women of integrity. When you demonstrate that you genuinely care for your staff, you will be amazed at what they will do or give up to serve God alongside you.

One of the pastors reporting to me walked into my office and said, "Blaine, I just got a call from such-and-such church. They just offered me five times what I am making here to come on board and be their youth pastor." Then he said, "I love it here! There is no way I could ever leave. No amount of money could ever buy me."

This is the kind of leadership you want to have on staff. Your leadership can cause people to climb mountains and cross rivers if you are a godly prototype.

3. Be a leader of excellence.

I believe every part of your life should exemplify an excellence that people want to follow. You need to be a leader at all times, not just when you show up at church and stand in the pulpit. You want to be a person people will follow regardless of what you are doing.

Many youth pastors feel being a good leader is being a spiritual person—praying, seeking God, and having great spiritual things to say. While that is a part of what you need to do to be effective, I believe you also need to stay ahead of the pack on all levels.

It is important to take care of your physical body and dress in a way that exemplifies your leadership. If you have an office, it ought to look sharp. You need to take care of your home and vehicle. Even the way you treat your spouse and children at home will make a difference in your leadership abilities in the church.

A Poor Example

I have been invited to preach at youth conferences across the United States. There have been times when the youth pastor who picked me up at the airport did not even bother to help with my bags. When we got to his car, it looked as though it had not been washed in months. The inside was filled with old McDonald's wrappers, and Happy Meal prizes were scattered throughout the car. Obviously, he was not expecting to pick me up, or he would have at least cleaned his car out. I thought, *Man, I cannot wait to see the church!*

When we walked into his office, there was stuff everywhere—all over the floor and scattered on his desk. He had some basketballs and volleyballs in the corner that were only half filled with air. He still had "See You At The Pole" promotional material from five years ago lying on top of his desk. The youth room was just like his office. Chairs were strewn all over the room. Even the banner with their logo on it was hanging lopsided on the wall.

It was no wonder he did not have many kids in his ministry! He did not conduct his life with any type of excellence. Who would want to be part of his ministry or want to follow that kind of leadership? Excellence has to be exhibited in every area of your life if you want to attract people who will follow and serve you in ministry.

4. Take risks and overcome failures.

You will have to be a risk-taker in order to succeed and be a great leader. Colonel Sanders, the creator of Kentucky Fried Chicken's famous secret recipe, was sixty-five years old when he began promoting his chicken recipe to restaurants across the U.S. and Canada. He wanted a nickel for every piece of chicken a restaurant sold using his special blend of eleven herbs and spices. He went to 1,009 businesses before he found someone to buy his recipe. Most people would have given up before they reached fifty restaurants, but he kept on going. He was not afraid of risk or failure. By 1964 he had successfully established six hundred franchises. Later that year, he sold his secret recipe to a group of investors for two million dollars!

Tom Landry, Chuck Nolan, and Bill Walsh account for nine of the sixteen Super Bowl victories between 1974 and 1989. They also had some of the worst records for first season head coaches in the NFL. Yet, they overcame their failures and went on to become some of the greatest coaches who ever lived.

Walt Disney went bankrupt seven times before he finally succeeded. How many people would have quit after two, three, or even four bankruptcies?

Clint Eastwood was fired in 1959 because he talked too slow, but that incident did not deter him. He went on to make his speech his trademark. It was the one thing that separated him from all the other actors of his day.

5. Be willing to confront areas and people that need to change.

To be a great leader you have to make changes when they need to be made. I work hard at training my leaders so they will be thoroughly equipped to do their jobs. You have to be willing to confront them if their departments are not working properly. If they refuse to improve and do the things they are asked to do, you have to make a change.

I have set high standards in all our departments. Sloppy work is not tolerated, and if a leader is doing something that causes young people not to return, it is dealt with immediately. Oneighty® began in 1995, and since that time, leadership has changed in at least six different departments. It is not easy to let someone go after you have invested time and training in him or her, but if you are going to be a strong leader you have to periodically change your leadership team so the entire department can grow.

Once you begin to develop cascading leadership, watch the number of teenagers attending your youth services soar. No one person can do everything. As you duplicate yourself in the lives of workers, you will discover your load is lighter. In the process, you will help others find their place in the body of Christ.

TOUGH QUESTIONS

Q: I don't have any leaders, and I'm desperate. Is it okay to lower our qualifications in the beginning to get things started?

A: Absolutely not. You have to stay strong in the qualifications you have for your workers. If you compromise your qualifications to a mediocre level, you set a low standard.

"Well, we'll let you come in. We know you're not really faithful to church, and that you're smoking on the side." That kind of compromise will cause you to lose the best of your people and ultimately the best of your students.

People love to be around ministries that have excellence. The kind of leaders you set in the beginning will be the kind of leaders you attract as you go further in ministry. If you have leadership that has been compromised, that is the kind of leaders you will draw. If you have excellence in leadership, you are going to draw other excellent leaders.

My philosophy is, I would rather start with five leaders who are really committed, faithful, and have great character, than fifty who will cause problems, possibly jeopardize our ministry, or do things to hurt our kids. Go for quality over quantity, even if it means you do it alone for the first few months until you finally get one or two quality people who can come in and help.

Q: I tell my leaders what to do, but they never seem to get it right. What am I doing wrong?

A: You may not be doing anything wrong; you may just need to go back and reaffirm the things you've asked them to do. People don't always get it right the first time; after all, they're human. It takes revisiting their area and working with them to get it right. You may want to look at the front end as well. Are you defining clearly what you want done? I also think it is important to model for them what you are asking them to do. Do it with them rather than just giving it to them.

When we started our drama ministry, I did not just give the drama team to my drama leader. I met with the drama team for the first several practices and helped them model how we would practice, how the skits would be done, and how the scripts would be written. Gradually I let go until I knew my drama leader could handle it by herself.

It also means making sure you delegate and model well on the front end, and then revisit that area to make sure it's up to par.

Q: I found out one of my key leaders was involved in sexual sin. He has asked forgiveness, repented, and wants to keep serving in ministry. Is that okay?

A: Well, I think it's okay that he asked for forgiveness, it's okay that he repented, and it's okay that he wants to serve in ministry; but no, you don't want to allow him to be in ministry right away. A double process needs to happen.

Number one, a healing and a strengthening process are necessary for those involved in sexual sin. Number two, they need to earn back your trust as a leader. Depending on the degree of involvement in sexual sin, you have to ask yourself if you would want to put them back in youth ministry.

If I had a leader who was involved in sexual sin with one of our students, I would probably never allow them back into youth ministry. I wouldn't be able to trust them again. If it was something else, maybe they were on the Internet checking out web pages they should not have been checking out, or some form of pornography, I would certainly set them down for a period.

Three to six months would be necessary to make sure they go through proper counseling, become strong, and completely recover. When I was in high school, I was on the junior varsity football team and I broke my arm the night before our championship game. I was doing something stupid. I was on the trampoline, and I should not have been. I broke my arm, and I hurt my team. I injured myself and took myself out of the game. I was a key player on the defense. I went to my team, I asked for for-giveness, and I said, "I'm sorry for doing this guys. I shouldn't have been doing this." But I was still injured and couldn't play the next day. If I had played it would have hurt my team and I certainly would have hurt my arm even more.

When people get involved in an area of sin like that, they have experienced a deep injury spiritually, and there must be sufficient time for complete and total restoration. That's an issue where you want to meet with your pastor and set up some time for the restoration process for them before you allow them back into ministry.

rule four:

Many people believe that if God speaks to their heart about something, everything will fall into place. Ministers may receive direction from God in a time of prayer or a prophecy in which God gives them direction for their ministry. They mistakenly think because He told them to do something, it will just happen. That is not true.

All the promises in the Bible do not automatically happen in our lives. We have a part to play in their manifestation. Yet, we hear people say, "I'm waiting on God for revival." If no one comes to church and no one is saved, they say, "Well, God just wasn't moving in the service today." This type of thinking comes from believing the fourth time-honored rule.

Rule Four: *A true move of God is never organized or programmed by men.*

I would like to submit that what most people refer to as a move of God is actually a move of man toward God. He has never taken a break nor has He had any momentary lapses of power. He does not move on your behalf when He *feels* like it. He does not arbitrarily choose to move in one church but not another. It is not a matter of God moving or not moving. It is a matter of men lining up with what He wants to do.

Moves of Men Toward God

The New Testament never talks about a move of God, but churchgoers and pastors alike will say, "We had a move of God in our church," or, "We are believing for a move of God in our city." When we make such statements, it sounds as though God moves sometimes but at other times He doesn't.

The book of Acts is filled with moves of men toward God. In Acts 16:25-26 Paul and Silas were placed in prison for preaching the gospel. After they "prayed, and sang praises unto God," (v. 25) suddenly there was an earthquake. It was only because they first moved toward God in worship and prayer that they were able to receive what was already available to them—their deliverance.

Another example is found in Acts 8:5-7. Phillip went to the city of Samaria to preach Christ to the Samaritans. After the people heard the gospel, "unclean spirits, crying with loud voices, came out of many that were possessed" (v. 7). If Phillip had not first gotten on his horse and traveled to Samaria, revival would not have broken out in that city. It was not a move of God toward the city of Samaria. It was a move of Phillip toward the plan of God.

Moses stretched out his hand over the Red Sea first; then God rolled the waters back. (Ex. 14:21.) Only after Joshua was obedient to God and commanded the children of Israel to march around the walls of Jericho did the walls come down. (Josh. 6:3-5, 20.) These are both moves of men toward God. Only after they moved first was God able to do what He wanted to do all along.

This erroneous rule has been followed for too long. It needs to be replaced with the following truth.

Truth Four: *Preparation paves the highway for the effective transport of the gospel to your target group.*

I have a sign in my office that reads, "If you sweat in preparation, you will not bleed in the battle." I would much rather sweat than bleed. I have passed this creed on to all my staff and have impressed upon them the importance of preparation. If I ever see one of them frantically running around fifteen minutes before a Wednesday night service, I know they are bleeding. They did not prepare properly. Many people in church leadership are bleeding instead of succeeding.

Preparation Time

First Corinthians 9:24 says, "Know ye not that they which run in a race run all, but one receiveth the prize? So run that ye may obtain." The gospel can be compared to a race. You cannot show up on the morning of a marathon race without any type of training and expect to win. Likewise, you have to spend the needed time to prepare before you preach the gospel.

Paul told us to have our "feet shod with the **preparation** of the gospel of peace" (Eph. 6:15). In other words, he was telling us never to preach the gospel without being prepared. In fact, you cannot effectively preach without the proper preparation.

Trying to minister to teenagers without careful thought, preparation, or organization would be like going to war in your bare feet. Soldiers would be ready to quit in just a few days. They would never succeed in battle.

God has always required a great deal of preparation in order to achieve great results. Look at Joseph. He had a dream when he was seventeen years old. The fulfillment of that dream came thirteen years later. Moses spent forty years in the land of Midian before God spoke to him about leading the nation of Israel.

Joshua was a young man when he spied out the land of Canaan. He spent forty years wandering in the wilderness as part of his training. At the age of eighty-five, he finally entered his ministry and led God's chosen people into the Promised Land.

David was a young lad of sixteen when he killed Goliath. He spent the next twenty-one years preparing for his leadership role as king over Israel. Some people incorrectly think the apostle Paul immediately became a pillar in the church after his Damascus road experience. He did not. He spent fourteen years in relative obscurity before he became a great leader in the early church. Even Jesus spent thirty years of preparation for three years of earthly ministry. If Jesus and these Old and New Testament patriarchs are our examples to follow, why do we think we can get by with little preparation?

Preparation time is never lost time. Young, on-fire workers may think they are ready to step out into ministry without the necessary training. This will only spell future disaster for them. Likewise, as you are preparing outreaches in your ministry, do not allow tight deadlines that skip the necessary preparation stage. When your plans begin to fall apart, you will wish you had taken the time to do more research and planning.

Eight Principles of the Miracle of Multiplication

Along with His many years of preparation, we can see a clear organization in the way Jesus ministered. Although He was often surrounded by a multitude, He did not minister in chaos. He took the time to organize the people before ministering to them.

A good example is recorded in Mark 6:32-44. Jesus was teaching a multitude in a desert place. As evening approached, the disciples told Him to send the people away so they could find food and lodging in the surrounding villages. Jesus said to them, "No, we need to feed them. What do *you* have to give them?" They had five loaves of bread and two fish. Jesus then instructed His disciples to sit the people down in groups of fifty. After He blessed the food, He gave it to His disciples to distribute among the people.

From this passage of Scripture we see how Jesus organized His leadership team as well as the multitude in order to receive the **miracle of multiplication.** Eight principles are found in Mark 6. If you follow them, you will experience multiplication in your ministry as well.

1. The multitude had a great need.

Jesus met a very natural need. The multitude was hungry, so He fed them. There was nothing spiritual about what He did. What are the needs you are trying to meet?

As a youth pastor, you must take time to study today's youth culture and find out what their needs are. You will find that when you address those needs, your outreach will quickly grow.

When Pastor George began to analyze the needs of young people, he found what they felt were their most important needs were different than what he thought. Most pastoral teams think that kids need spiritual help, that they need Jesus. And certainly, that is true. Teenagers, however, think their biggest need is a social need. They want to be accepted. They do not go to roller skating rinks to skate or to an arcade to play games. If it were about roller-skating or playing games, they could do both at home. They go out to meet people and socialize.

It is sometimes hard to admit, but many kids do not come to Oneighty® to hear me preach. A few may come to solely hear the Word. However, most come because their need for social activity is met. Thank God, they hear the preaching of the Word every Wednesday night, but I am not the main drawing point of Oneighty®. Once we get them here, we can begin to redirect their priorities.

To meet the social needs of our teenagers, we simply asked ourselves, "What do they like to do?" The answer was very simple. They like to eat, hang out, and play games. Therefore, we incorporated these as a part of our environment. As we began to meet their social needs, the multitudes began to come.

2. Jesus had a compassion that moved Him to act.

Compassion is an intense desire to meet needs. Just because you know about a need does not mean the situation will change. If you are not motivated to do anything, young people will not be helped. You have to have love and compassion for teenagers in order to reach them. Compassion will cause you to wake up in the morning thinking about them. Without it, your ministry will not last.

You may have started out with compassion to reach young people. However, in your ministry efforts to reach them, you may feel burned out. You can rekindle your compassion simply by spending time with the Lord. Time alone with God is necessary. Although you are constantly studying the Word in preparation for your sermons, you must never neglect reading and studying the Word for yourself. There is a difference between the two. By spending time with the Lord to build yourself up, you will not experience "burn out."

3. Jesus used what His team had to give.

He asked His disciples in Mark 6, "What do you have?" They told Him they had some bread. He said, "Good, we will start with that." He found out what talents and abilities His team had and went from there.

When people enroll in our Leadership Training Institute, we interview them to find out where their skills lie and in what areas they would like to serve. We then focus on developing their gifts. They may not always start in the area of their choice, but we have a starting point from which to work. If a leadership student is good at sound, he or she will not immediately start working in the Oneighty® sound department. Instead, that individual will be placed in our junior high sound department to grow and develop there.

4. Jesus commanded the multitude to sit down.

This is a preparation stage. Neither Jesus nor His disciples could have fed all five thousand people at one time. To effectively minister to that many people, preparation had to come first. They could not properly assess the situation with the crowd standing up and moving around. Jesus, therefore, commanded everyone to sit down.

5. He divided them into ranks of fifty and one hundred.

By doing this, the multitude was broken into manageable groups. This was to make sure the needs of all the people were equally met. The disciples could not have *individually* ministered to five thousand people, and neither can you. By following Jesus' example and dividing large numbers into smaller groups, you will be able to effectively minister to a multitude of teenagers.

6. Jesus released His disciples to distribute bread.

This stage involves delegation. By Himself, Jesus could not have handed out bread to five thousand people. After He blessed the bread, He broke it and gave it to His disciples to distribute. His disciples became His hands and feet. In the same way, the more you delegate to your trained ministers, the more kids you will be able to reach.

7. They witnessed the miracle of multiplication.

Up until this point, the disciples did all the work. Now it was time for God to do the miraculous among them. However, if they had not completed steps one through six, God would not have been able to multiply what they had done.

8. They collected the baskets of leftovers.

After their work was done, they reaped the harvest of their efforts. I want you to see that for every miracle you receive, you have to do seven out of the eight steps. God has only one part. He does the miraculous. You have a much bigger role to play than He does. Only after you have completed your part is He able to step in and multiply your efforts. If you slack off in your preparation and eliminate some of these steps, your harvest will be minimal rather than bountiful.

Giving Away the Ministry

This may sound contrary to traditional thinking, but instead of holding on to your youth ministry, consider giving away its ownership. What do I mean by this? Simply delegate facets of the ministry to others. When you do this, you create a sense of ownership among your workers and students. You are actually giving them an opportunity to run with your vision. By accepting ownership, they are accepting the responsibility to bring it to pass.

Something happens in people's attitudes when they take ownership. They treat it differently. You will love, protect, and care for something that is yours. Have you ever rented a car? I rent one when I travel. I have to be honest, though. I do not treat a rental car the same way I treat my own car.

I have never checked the oil in any of the cars I have rented, nor do I clean them before turning them in. I have also been known not to slow down when going over speed bumps! I do not abuse the car, but it is not my responsibility to maintain a rental car. However, if I were a part owner in a rental car company, I would treat the cars differently. I would take better care of the cars and I would not drive as fast over the speed bumps.

Ownership changes a person's attitude. Your students will treat the youth ministry differently when they feel they have part ownership of it. They will give of their time and finances as well as their sweat. They will do whatever it takes to see the ministry grow because it belongs to them.

TOUGH QUESTIONS

Q: I'm not a very organized person. Do you have any suggestions?

A: Well, you and I should get together because I am not very organized either. I have learned to surround myself with organized people. Wherever you are weak, and we all have weaknesses, add to yourself the strengths you need in other people.

That is why God gave us the body of Christ. He knew we couldn't do it alone and needed one another. He has forced us to work together, and it's a team ministry. There should be one leader. We know anything that has multiple heads is a monster, right? That leader is not going to have it all; he is not going to know it all or be able to do it all.

Learn to surround yourself with people who can help you get better organized.

Q: I've heard you won't hire someone who doesn't tithe. Why are you so tough in this area?

A: That is true. Before we hire someone on staff in any area of Oneighty® or our church, we check their tithing records. Obviously, they have to be a member of our church. We check records to see if they have been faithful and consistent in giving. We actually ask that question in the interview process, but we also verify it.

The Bible says when we don't tithe, we rob God. (Mal. 3:8.) It is very simple; if someone will steal from God, they will rob you. They will hurt you. Jesus said this in the Gospels: If you are not faithful with unrighteous mammon, how will you ever be given true riches? (Luke 16:11.)

If someone isn't faithful in giving 10 percent back to the Lord that belongs to Him, then how are you going to trust him or her with the souls of young people? We are very careful in this area.

We want to be sure people are obedient, not only in the tithe but in every area of their life, before they join our team. They are going to be leaders that lead your entire team and all your students. If they are walking in disobedience in certain areas, that is going to be passed on in your ministry.

Q: If you "draft" your workers, won't you get people who really don't want to serve, but rather feel obligated?

A: I don't believe that. Jesus drafted all twelve of His disciples, and they stayed with Him, except for one. You may lose one or two along the way, but for the most part people are going to catch your heart, your vision, and the vision of the ministry and respond to that.

I was drafted early in ministry. I had people call me into ministry and ask me to do things at first I did not think I would like or enjoy. But as I got into it and began to see the opportunity to help young people, my heart grew warm and I really enjoyed doing it. You are going to keep most of those you draft, and they will serve you a long time as you lead and motivate them correctly.

the oneighty® organization

We have developed a solid organizational structure for Oneighty® that is constantly being tweaked. Ministries are added as we grow, and departments that are not working are removed. As you study our operations, adapt the information and ideas to work in your youth ministry.

There are two flow charts in my office. One chart shows how our organization is currently established. The second one is a visionary flowchart. It contains the structure for the ideas I want to implement down the road. It is good to set future goals. When you know where you are headed, you can better plan how to get there. Along the way, look for faithful people to fill positions when the time comes.

Weekly Ministries

We chose to hold Oneighty® every Wednesday night because it proved to be the day attendance was the highest. We have tried other nights of the week. We found out that on Saturday nights Christian kids would come, but the unsaved kids we wanted to reach would go to parties. We were asking them to choose between going to parties and meeting cool-looking girls, or going to church and listening to some guy preach. In most cases, they went to parties.

Wednesday night works best. It is a school night, and young people love to get out on a school night. Most parents will allow their teenagers to go out on a weeknight when they are going to church. When you give unsaved teenagers the choice of attending a church filled with all kinds of video games or staying home to do their homework, the choice is easy to make. They will come to Oneighty®.

Team Oneighty® Bible studies are on Monday night every two weeks. These are training, teaching, and discipleship meetings held in the homes of our teenagers. They gather to study the Word, worship, and strategize their campus ministry.

Our junior high ministry is called Genesis, and services are held during our weekend church services. This service is more informal than the Wednesday night services, and usually between 100 and 125 young people attend each of our three weekend services at Church On The Move. The smaller groups allow for more one-on-one time with the teens.

Junior high is a critical time for young people. They need as much attention as you can give. The twelve- through fourteen-year-old age range is the period when they decide how they are going to live their lives. They are developing their identity. At this age, they are deciding what kind of person they are going to be.

The sixteen- through eighteen-year-olds are really a product of the decisions they made when they were younger. We, therefore, work hard with the junior high kids to disciple them in the things of the Lord so they will make godly lifestyle choices.

Our high school students attend the adult church service and sit under Pastor George. This is designed to keep them part of the local church. The game room is not open on Sundays or after school. If Oneighty® were located right across the street from a high school campus, we might have an after-school program where they could come in and hang out. There are several Oneighty® affiliate programs that do this, but our Oneighty® facility is located in an industrial park, miles from any neighborhood or public high school campus.

Oneighty® Staff

Pastor George is at the head of the organizational chart. The vision and ministry to the youth began with him. He is ultimately responsible for everything we do. I report to Pastor George and manage the entire operation of Oneighty®. My assistant youth pastor is responsible for many of the organizational details of the ministry.

Apprentices and Interns

An apprentice is a second-year intern or someone who has graduated from internship. They have the opportunity to get more experience through a second year of training and ministry. An intern is either a recent graduate from high school or someone in his or her early twenties. The goals of interns vary. Some want to serve in the area of helps by learning how to develop administrative and leadership skills. Others are training to be youth pastors, youth leaders, campus ministers, evangelists, or missionaries.

After acceptance into the yearlong program, individuals are required to raise their own financial support. Our program is different in that no fee is charged to work in the ministry. In fact, our interns receive a small amount of spending money each month. Our apprentices and interns help in every area of the ministry. The one- to two-year program is a time of intense training. We pour our heart into them to develop well-grounded leaders.

Office Set-Up

Each Wednesday we hold a weekly one-hour prayer and direction meeting. We pray for upcoming events and all the different outreaches in Oneighty®. The Wednesday meetings are also a time of leadership training. We discuss what was done in the previous week and alter anything that was not working well. I also give the staff direction for the week.

I have regular one-on-one meetings with all the volunteer department leaders. I want to be informed on how things are going for them. The meetings serve as a time for me to build up and edify my volunteer workers.

Building Staff Unity

It is important to have regular staff parties and excursions in order to build good chemistry with your staff and essential leadership roles. Have fun with your workers. Once my team and I engaged in some friendly combat on a paint ball course. We have also played laser-tag and gone bowling, among other activities. Fun time with your staff is an easy way to develop relationships.

Recognition Awards

Members of our staff team have the opportunity to receive one of three different recognition awards in our weekly meetings:

The Excellence Award: This is awarded when someone is doing a first-class job on a project.

The Great-Idea Award: As the name implies, this is a trophy passed around for great ideas. It is not passed around every week, only when someone comes up with an idea that actually works. Then the "great idea" recipient is publicly acknowledged.

The "Ha" Award: (meaning, "Ha," you messed up!) I found a trophy that is just the rear end of a horse. Whenever someone messes up in the office, they will be presented with the "Ha" Award. Everyone eventually gets it so no one feels like he or she is being singled out. If one person makes a mistake, we all want to learn from it so the same mistake is not repeated.

Top 25 Office Resolutions

My staff has a "Top 25" list of guidelines on day-in and day-out operations. Much of this list is simple, common courtesy and goes a long way in developing camaraderie among the staff.

1. Return all telephone calls. That is so simple, but many times it does not happen.

2. Use your energy and your intelligence as if all results depend only on you.

3. Give recognition and credit as if all results depend only on others.

4. Support and make your boss or department leader look good in public. Provide feedback in private.

5. Remember to say "please" and "thank you."

6. For every complaint you make, have a possible solution or recommendation.

7. Never miss a deadline. If it looks like you are going to be late, negotiate and change the deadline. If you cannot change it, get help.

8. Find out whether your telephone calls are welcome or intrusive. When you call someone, ask, "Is this a good time to talk?"

9. Communicate with eye contact. Always look people in the eye, whether you are involved in a heavy negotiation or handing off an assignment to a staff member.

10. Solicit criticism and accept it without being defensive. Be willing to ask people, "Am I doing a good job? How can I improve?"

11. Never be afraid to say "I'm sorry" or "I apologize."

12. Before beginning any discussion, clearly state the purpose, desired outcome, and key objective.

13. Keep up-to-date on the latest technology. Learn as much as you can about new developments.

14. Do not guess or assume if you do not know.

15. Keep the inside and outside of your car clean. Dark colors show more dust in California, light colors in Pittsburgh. Since we are in Oklahoma, it does not matter much.

16. Raise everyone's educational and interest level by distributing timely articles or quotations. We have a magnetic board where we post articles and other neat things.

17. Do not promise performance unless you can deliver.

18. Admit your error immediately. Report it to the person who can solve it or repair it quickly.

19. Keep a neat and tidy office and desk. A messy environment could influence a person's perception of you.

20. Always write a personal thank-you note within two days for special favors.

21. Answer the telephone within three rings.

22. If you ever doubt an action, apply the television test. Would you be comfortable if what you are doing were broadcast on the six o'clock news?

23. Once you ask a question, be quiet and let the other person talk.

24. Before entering serious negotiations, decide which issues you are willing to give on.

25. Keep your boss in the loop; let him or her know what you are doing. Always apply the "no surprise" rule.

Boxes, Memos, and Calendars

A calendar is distributed every month to all workers, both paid and volunteer. It includes all activities at Oneighty® and allows everyone to be informed and know the agenda for the month. Each worker also has a box for memos and any miscellaneous information we distribute to staff and volunteers. Our main communication is through memos. It is much easier to type a memo and put it in everyone's box than to reach staff and volunteers by telephone to relay information. We use e-mail as well, but not every staff member has a computer.

Adult Workers Only

In the different areas of ministry at Oneighty®, we discovered some ministries are more effective if an adult worker is in place. We *only* permit adult workers in the following areas.

1. Ushers. (A disruptive student will not listen to another student when told to be quiet in the service.)

2. Bus Drivers. (A student is not permitted to drive a bus.)

3. Parking.

4. Security.

5. Game room monitors. The monitors serve in certain areas of the game room to make sure nothing gets out of hand.

6. Bookstore workers.

7. Discipleship check-in and checkout.

8. Hospitality. Since we hold two back-to-back services on Wednesday nights, volunteers organize finger foods and drinks so the workers can get a bite to eat between each service.

9. Oneighty® Mobile Rewards program. We only allow adults to drive the Oneighty® Mobile and pick up students.

10. Ministry Department Directors. Anyone who is over a ministry at Oneighty®—ushers, counselors, greeters, etc.—must be an adult.

Adult or Teenager Ministries

Both adults and teenagers may be involved in the following ministries with the exception of greeter, which is designated only for teenagers.

1. Greeters. (Teenagers only.)

2. Altar counselors. (Consists of adults and teenagers who have gone through training.)

3. Music ministry, singers and musicians.

4. Audio and video teams.

5. Café workers.

6. Campus Ministry. Adults oversee the program, but teenagers conduct the actual campus ministry.

7. Mission teams.

8. Juvenile Prison Ministry. Adults oversee the program. Students are involved in every aspect of the ministry from worship to teaching and testifying.

9. Drama team.

10. Work projects. (Includes workdays at Dry Gulch, the Oneighty® facility, and Church On The Move.)

11. New visitor follow-up programs.

12. Information booth. This is a place where young people can register for camp, mission trips, etc. They can also get information about current activities.

Drafting Workers

Jesus did not wait for volunteers. He drafted workers. Notice in Matthew 4:19 He said, "Follow me, and I will make you fishers of men." There is a difference between drafting and asking for help. People respond better when you present an opportunity that benefits them in some way. Eight ways to draft workers for your ministry are listed below to assist you in your drafting efforts.

1. Preach vision and not need.

People are vision-motivated, not need-motivated. You can get up and say, "We need help. Just look at the needs of today's teenagers. They are on drugs and are going to hell. Please help us." People may feel sorry for you, but they probably will not be motivated to help you. When you tell them you are taking over high school campuses with the gospel and kids are being saved by the hundreds, then they will want to be part of what you are doing. You are not preaching need; you are preaching vision.

2. Promise benefits.

When we draft workers, we show people how it will benefit them. Jesus said, "If you follow Me, I will make you something." (Matt. 4:19.) He was saying by working with Him, He would make them into leaders who would influence others.

3. Show enthusiasm and excitement.

People respond to someone who is excited about what he or she is doing.

4. Have people respond publicly in services.

When people commit publicly, they are more likely to follow through and show up.

5. Use your church bulletin.

If you have a church bulletin, advertise your youth program as well as any special event you are holding. Whenever I really need some help in a certain area, I will send a short memo to Pastor George asking him to give this area a verbal plug on Sunday morning.

6. Recruit when you are conducting leadership meetings.

Whenever you are holding a leadership meeting with your current staff and volunteers, invite people in the church to come and see what is going on. Then have applications ready for them if they want to sign up.

7. Give public recognition to current leaders.

The Walt Disney Company has 180 different recognition programs. The more you recognize people who are serving you, the more they will want to continue serving you. Throughout the summer, Pastor George gives away $50 and $100 Outback Steakhouse gift certificates to extremely faithful workers. It is a small way of saying we appreciate all they are doing.

8. Encourage current leaders to use their network of relationships to draft for you.

All our workers have a network of probably fifteen to twenty good relationships. We encourage them to tap into their network of friends to recruit for Oneighty®.

Qualifying Workers

Any new worker has to first attend our Leadership Training Institute. They listen to three weeks of audiotapes and fill out an accompanying worksheet. The first tape goes over our vision. The second tape covers the qualifications we look for in youth workers. The third tape explains how to become a good leader. By going through a training program, we do not have to constantly re-train every single person who comes in.

All new volunteers are required to fill out an application. From it, we learn about their former church membership. They also give us references from people who will vouch for their character. We find out what kind of ministry experience they might have and where their talents lie.

If I see on the application that an individual has been a member of three different churches in the last ninety days, I know we have a problem. We require every person to attend Church On The Move for six months before applying for helps ministry. We want to know they will stick around and not quit right after we have trained them.

One of the qualifications for our youth program is that a person does not smoke. If someone applies who does smoke, we will ask him or her to first quit smoking. When they have not smoked for at least three months, they can come back and re-apply.

You have to hold your standard of leadership high. You should not lower your standard to accept workers. Make a point to look for people with character and integrity. If you don't, you will not have a good program.

We do background checks on all our applicants. We check to see if they have a criminal record, especially child molestation. If they have a record, we want to know. We have learned from the background checks of some of our applicants that they had recently been arrested for drunk driving. They do not need to be serving in ministry. They need to be sitting in church where they can learn and grow.

Here are some red flags that will alert you to unfaithful workers:

1. Multiple church attendance background

These people have not been faithful to any one church but have bounced from church to church. You want to find out why they never stayed long with any one church.

2. Not attending church services

People cannot spend all their time giving without being fed. If one of your workers never shows up to adult church when he or she is not working in the youth ministry, you have to encourage him or her to be fed regularly.

3. Not a tither

People who do not tithe do not honor God. If they do not honor God, what makes you think they will honor you? This is a very important matter, and we check the tithing records of our key volunteer workers and all our staff.

4. Home life is not in order

If any aspect of a person's home life is not in order—marital problems, alcohol or drug abuse—we ask that individual to get straightened out before he or she begins to serve or continues serving.

5. Gossips about previous churches

If an individual constantly gossips about his or her previous church, he or she will soon be talking about you. We do not put up with gossip. We will not ask people to leave, but we will insist they stop gossiping or step down.

6. Counsels one-on-one with teenagers

We do not permit any one-on-one ministry. We only permit two-on-one. If a young person needs personal guidance, we require two adults to be part of the guidance session. We do this for a worker's protection and safety. Too many things can happen. It is always a good idea to have someone else in the room to witness what you said.

7. Consistently late for meetings and assignments

When people are always late, it tells us they do not value what they are doing.

8. Raises constant concerns about your doctrine or leadership

Amos 3:3 says, "Can two walk together, except they be agreed?" If someone is working with you but does not believe in where you are going or what your leadership philosophy is, you need to deal with that person. They will hurt your ministry, not help it.

9. Not willing to do something small

If people are not interested in starting in an insignificant area to prove their faithfulness, we are not interested in trying them out in an area with a lot of responsibility.

10. Talks title rather than responsibility

We are not interested in people who are looking for titles. We want people who want to serve.

As you study our organizational structure, you may not be ready for some areas. Use what will fit in your current church structure.

A lot of team building boils down to respecting one another. As you make a point to show your staff and volunteers that you appreciate what they are doing, your team will be loyal and dedicated workers.

rule five:

DO NOT ATTRACT KIDS AWAY FROM OTHER YOUTH GROUPS IN YOUR CITY

Our goal at Oneighty® is to make it hard for the teenagers in our city to go to hell. We want to reach any young person who is headed that way. Our goal is not to pull teenagers away from their youth groups. We are going after the unsaved and unchurched kids. However, if what you are doing has quality to it, it is inevitable that you will attract both saved and unsaved young people.

Rule Five: *Do not attract kids away from other youth groups in your city.*

There is a difference between attracting and recruiting. I have never gone to other churches to recruit teenagers. People make choices every day about where they will attend church. They base their choices on what they expect to receive, how they are treated, and how they can get involved. The more young people can get involved and enjoy what they are doing, the more they will come. In the process, you will draw teens from other churches as well.

I have been asked if I get a lot of grief from youth pastors whose teenagers have left their group to come to Oneighty®. The answer is yes. If this happens to you, take a good look at what you are doing.

Not all the teens who come to Oneighty® stay. I have heard many reasons for people leaving. Some have gone to smaller youth groups where they are more recognized. Others have gone to ministries where they worship longer than we do. When I hear these reasons, I do not get upset at the other youth ministries. I look at what we are doing to see if we can make improvements.

How can we make Oneighty® more personal? Is there any way we can increase our worship? If we can improve, then I will make the necessary changes. However, if someone leaves because of a difference of philosophy, I keep doing what I am doing.

I cannot change my philosophy for every person who leaves just because they did not like something.

I also do everything I can to repair bridges and build relationships with other youth pastors. If I hear someone is upset with me, I will call and talk to him or her. I have developed several good relationships with other youth pastors this way. I am not trying to compete with other churches. My competition is the world and everything the devil uses to lure young people away from God.

Working Together

The disciples saw someone casting out devils using the name of Jesus. Because he was not part of their group, they forbid him from continuing to do so. When they told Jesus, He said, "Forbid him not: for there is no man which shall do a miracle in my name, that can lightly speak evil of me" (Mark 9:39).

Sometimes I think youth pastors believe there are not enough unsaved kids to go around. When I was a pastor in Colorado Springs, a survey was done to find out how many unchurched people lived there. One aspect of the survey was to find out how the churches in the city would be able to handle a major revival. I was shocked with the results. The survey showed the churches in Colorado Springs could only hold approximately 23-37 percent of the population.[1]

Before the survey, I thought Colorado Springs was a Christianized city. Although there are 15-20 nationally known ministries in the city, there are well over 100 of them altogether. It surprised me to discover how many people did not have a personal relationship with the Lord.

The ministers in Colorado Springs realized they needed help. When a new church came to the city, they did not feel threatened but welcomed them. I encourage you to look at your city in light of what Jesus told His disciples. If your fellow ministers are not against you, then they are for you.

Matthew 25 tells the story of the unfaithful servant. This servant did not multiply his talent but rather dug up the ground and hid it. When the master came back, he said:

> Take therefore the talent from him, and give it unto him which hath ten talents. For unto every one that hath shall be given, and he shall have abundance: but from him that hath not shall be taken away even that which he hath (vv.28,29).

Jesus wants us to develop our talents and use them to bring an increase to the body of Christ. Those who do not grow will end up losing what they have. When a church is not doing much with their young people, the Holy Spirit will draw these teenagers to a place where they can grow.

We are not competing with any church. God will bless anyone who applies His principles of growth to his or her organization.

Truth Five: *Build and promote a youth ministry that will appeal to all teenagers and allow them to discover the joy of living for Christ.*

I want to encourage you to gear your program toward more than just what Christians do. Most youth pastors design their ministry for the "on-fire, totally radical, sold-out" Christian kid. They keep the core group of teens pumped up, edified, and challenged, but the rest of their teenagers are ignored. Meanwhile, we talk and preach about reaching the lost but rarely do anything practical to bring them in.

Reaching the Unsaved and Unchurched

We have purposed to mobilize our core students to go after the lukewarm, middle-of-the-road student and reach the unchurched and unsaved young person.

We used to get up every week and ask our kids to please bring their friends. However, after we began working on what we had to offer them, we found we did not have to beg anymore. They bring their friends because they are proud of what we do and how our facility looks. Many teens are ashamed of their church. They would love to get their friends saved, but their church youth program is too hokey. They are not sure their friends would be saved or even want to come back after the first visit.

We developed a program both saved and unsaved kids want to attend. We have just as many churched as unchurched teenagers who come. Now we have to figure out where to put all the people they bring. If you put together a good program, your teens will bring their unchurched friends without your asking.

The Ministry Participation Processes

Our outreach to young people ministers to them regardless of their spiritual maturity. Understanding our illustration of the different levels in a football stadium will help you reach teenagers who are at various stages of spiritual development and growth.

At the top of the stadium are the community students. These young people live in your city. They might have heard about the game (your youth program). They may have even attended a game or two, or they might not even know it exists.

As a church, we have a responsibility to reach our community and not just minister to the teenagers who already come to our church. Jesus wants us to go after the lost. He compared it to the man who left the ninety-nine sheep to go after one that was lost. (Matt. 18:12-13.) The vision you have to reach the community will be completely different from how you minister to your core Christian young people.

Then you have the casual fans. They have paid only a couple of dollars for the seats in the peanut gallery. They are not committed to the ball club, or they would have paid more money for good seats. Casual fans do not come every week. You see them when someone invites them. Once at the game, they do not watch it closely. They will eat popcorn and talk to their friends, but they are not into the game. They only check it out every now and then.

Everyone has casual fans in their youth group. They are kids who could not care less about your message. They are not there to cheer you on, and in some cases would rather be somewhere else. We have kids like that every week in Oneighty®. If they keep coming, we have a plan to reach them.

Next are the season ticket holders who are really into the game. They sit on the front row and believe in what you are doing. They bring their Bibles every week and participate during the worship service. After the service, they tell you what a great job you are doing. We all love those kids. We thank God for them on the way home every night!

Finally, you have the players. These people are there early and stay late. They help you clean up the youth room, greet, and go on mission trips. Players are involved and believe in everything you are doing.

Every week you will have students from each of these groups attend your youth service. The challenge is to develop a program that ministers to all levels of spiritual growth.

The Community Student

Reaching the community student begins with prayer. Then you have to come up with a strategy to minister to them. Our strategy was to invite every student in junior high and high school to Oneighty®. That was how we came up with the idea to put together the Oneighty® invitation.

We also wanted Oneighty® to become a household name. We placed commercial spots on radio stations that had large teen audiences. We advertised on a billboard that was in a strategic location outside a major mall in Tulsa. For two years, any teenager who went to the mall had to drive by the billboard. The billboard had only our logo and a short description of what we are. They may not have known everything about Oneighty®, but at least our name was branded into their heads.

We worked hard to let the community know we exist. Today our name is recognized throughout Tulsa. Our local newspaper and three of the major TV networks in Tulsa have interviewed us. CBS' *Early Show* with Bryant Gumbel did a national story on the

"Oneighty® Phenomenon." Only on rare occasions do I meet someone who has not heard about Oneighty®.

The Casual Fan

The Oneighty® discipleship program is designed to reach the casual fan. When teenagers come forward during an altar call, we pray with them and take them into our counseling room. At that point, we get them plugged into the discipleship program. (More information about the discipleship program can be found in Chapter 11.) This program moves a casual fan from a back seat to the next level of growth.

We have found that after young people go through the eight-week discipleship program and take the zero pledge, we can get them involved in different ministry programs. (More information about the zero pledge can be found in Chapter 11.) An important element for their growth is to get them plugged in right away.

The Season Ticket Holder

The season ticket holder is an easy step away from getting involved in ministry. They are already excited about what you are doing. You just have to ask them to serve in the ministry or go on a mission trip. If you give them an opportunity to serve, they are ready to jump in and help.

Youth Meetings to Reach All Levels

Everything we do is analyzed to be effective in reaching teenagers at every stadium level. You can use the following ten steps to develop a youth program that will draw young people to your youth ministry.

1.   Make a strong first impression.

Studies have shown that people decide in the first twelve minutes whether or not they will come back to a church.1 When I heard this, I thought, **They have not even heard from me in the first twelve minutes.** I thought their decision to return had everything to do with my charismatic personality and dynamic communication skills, but it has nothing to do with me.

When newcomers visit Oneighty®, they see our parking lot attendants, greeters, and "Adore," our worship band, in the first twelve minutes. Their first impression, therefore, depends on the team I have in place. When I realized this, I began to work on those twelve minutes.

We started in the parking lot. We focused on organization and safety to the outside area of the building. We do not permit speeding or drag racing. A security team is in place, and they patrol the parking lot the entire night. This lets teenagers know we are in control and they will not be able to get away with anything. We leave a strong impression on both parents and teenagers. Therefore, parents are not afraid to drop their children because it looks too chaotic outside the building.

Friendly teenagers welcome newcomers to Oneighty®. We use only teens in the position of greeter. If you use adult greeters, you leave the impression that you are pretending to be a youth group. Upbeat music is playing as they enter the facility.

In looking around, first-time visitors will not think they are in church. Anything that can be considered religious has been removed. The facility is fun and inviting. There is a lot of color and activity. The first few minutes of the worship service are filled with high energy and embrace today's youth culture.

Most of the time kids want to come back although they may not come every week. Many kids call Oneighty® their home church but come only once or twice a month. Our goal is to get them here every time the door opens.

I once met a teenager at the ice rink. His parents do not go to any church, and he only makes it to Oneighty® once a month. Yet, he considers us his church. Keep in mind the number of teens who call your youth group home may be much higher than your actual weekly attendance. Newcomers may not come back every single week, but they will come back again if you make a good, strong first impression.

2. Keep your services moving quickly.

Today's teenagers are mosaic not linear learners. By that I mean they can learn while more than one thing is going on at a time. Adults are generally linear learners. Linear learners like to do only one thing at a time. They watch TV, listen to the radio, listen to a tape, or read a book. They do not combine activities.

Teenagers are not like that. My middle son is a mosaic learner. He will have headphones on but is listening to the music only in one ear because he is talking on the telephone with the other ear. The TV will be on, but it is muted, so he is only watching the pictures. At the same time, he is doing his homework assignment in English.

If you try to have a linear youth meeting—slow, predictable, and unimaginative—they will get bored quickly. Teenagers want things to be moving and happening all the time. To keep their attention, your meetings have to be popping.

3. Think beyond your Christian kids in planning services.

When you plan your worship service, keep in mind that the unchurched and unsaved kids will not enjoy long extended periods of worship. They do not know what worship is. To them, it is weird to sing to God for a half-hour. To anyone who grew up in the church or who has made a commitment to Christ, it is normal. It is uncomfortable for an unchurched kid to sing to a God they do not know.

I explain from time to time why we worship God. I never assume all the young people who come to the service know. When some of our students lift their hands during worship, the unchurched kids look around and wonder what in the world is going on. Before I start to preach, I will take a few moments to explain what the Christian kids are doing.

The gifts of the Spirit operate in our services regularly. Any time the Spirit of God moves in the service, I will explain what is happening for the sake of the unchurched teenagers, especially after tongues and interpretation. They might think I just decided to speak in Chinese for a little bit. They do not have any idea of what is going on. I always take the time to explain so they will gain understanding.

4. Distribute a meeting schedule to all participants with time limits.

Our services on Wednesday nights are about an hour long. Every minute of the service is planned. Here is a sampling of how our service might be put together.

1. The "Rules" video (explains what they can and can't do!) —one minute

2. DJ intro music—one minute

3. Open up and welcome first time visitors—seven minutes

4. Announcements—five minutes

5. Two upbeat praise songs—seven minutes

6. Offering—three minutes

7. Two to three worship songs—ten minutes

8. Ministry time after worship—three minutes

9. Video of some kind—two minutes (We do not have a video every week, but on occasion we will do some kind of video skit or promo.)

10. Drama skit—five minutes (Usually we do a live drama, but sometimes we will have a video drama.)

11. Message—twenty minutes

12. Altar call—five minutes

13. Final exhortation and dismissal—one minute

We usually allow a few minutes in our schedule for what we call "transition fluff." Someone always goes over his or her allotted time, so we allow for that.

Everyone involved in the service receives a schedule. They know exactly how much time they have for their portion of the service. I am the only one who can change the schedule. You can have multiple participants in a service, but you cannot have multiple leaders. If the worship needs to go longer, God will speak to me. I will then direct the worship leader to keep singing.

As a leader, you need to sit down with your people and define their time limits. If you do not, you will have a long, drawn-out service because everyone will take more time than they should. Sometimes I have one of my staff members run a stopwatch during the service. I receive a written report with how long each part of the service took. If someone went over their time, I will tell them to pay closer attention in the next service.

5. Develop a worship ministry that captures the heart of a teenager.

We begin with a time of praise. We usually sing a couple hand-clapping, energetic praise songs. Later we sing slower worship songs and encourage every student to enter in.

I encourage you to keep your worship short. There is no scriptural mandate that says you **have** to worship for an hour. In fact, during the Last Supper, Jesus had the most important meeting of His ministry. When He concluded speaking to His disciples, they sang a hymn and left. (Matt. 26:30.) They did not sing for an hour or even fifteen minutes. They sang one hymn and moved on to something else.

I want our teens to leave wanting more. I have kids coming up to me from time to time, saying, "Blaine, I wish our worship was longer." I would rather hear that than, "Blaine, I wish our worship was shorter," or "I wish you would preach shorter!"

I tell them worship on Wednesday night is just an appetizer for the main course. I encourage them to develop a worshiping lifestyle in their daily walk with God. Worship does not have to stop once they leave the building. A lifestyle of worship begins by worshiping God on the way to school and continuing until you go to bed at night.

Psalm 47:1 instructs us to clap our hands and shout to God. During worship, our worship leader will draw the young people in to participate with brief moments of encouragement between or before songs. Sometimes students refuse to participate during the praise service because they are not sure of what other students might say. It is up to the worship leader to come against any type of hindrance by encouraging everyone to join in.

It is important that the songs are sung in a key that is comfortable for teenagers. I have seen worship leaders sing in high keys that make their voices sound good. However, half of the kids cannot reach the high notes. This may demand your worship leader adjust his or her comfort level of singing. If the teenage boys can sing comfortably, you are in a key that the majority of your students will be able to sing in as well. Most girls can sing high, but if you sing in a key all the girls can sing in, none of the guys will be able to sing. Then you will lose everyone, because for the most part, girls follow guys.

The worship team meets every week to develop their skills and work on songs. Today we write most of our own worship songs, but it did not start out that way. It takes time to find the right people and build a solid worship team. You have to start with what you have. If you are the only one to sing, then sing with all your heart. You do not have to start out with a band if you do not have musicians. Get some tracks and go for it! Many ministries have been there and done that. Start where you are and believe God to bring in musicians.

Encourage your worship leader to lead from the heart. Worship leaders need to have a passion about worshiping God. Their passion will carry over to the young people during the worship service and get them going too.

Take the time to find out what styles of music your kids like. We took a survey among our youth group to find out what radio stations they listened to. With that information, we knew the kind of music they liked. We then incorporated that style of music in our worship service. Our worship is different than most worship services, but we use the style of music the kids like.

6. Use video to promote new events and relive past ones.

We are ministering to a TV generation. Video announcements are easy to do. It is relatively inexpensive to buy a digital home video camera and a home editing system. We promote many of our upcoming events on video.

We also use video to relive past events. At the end of our mission trips, we take a powerful Christian song and make a music video that contains the highlights of the trip. We play it for the adult church as well as for our teenagers. It is a powerful way to relive those experiences. Try to use video at least once a month.

7. Use drama as an icebreaker to set the theme for your message.

We use drama three to four times a month. On the off weeks, we will show a video or illustrate a message. I give the drama coordinator topics for at least eight messages at a time. They are not necessarily the sermons written out, but I usually know the topics I want to preach two months in advance.

The dramas are designed to reinforce the sermon. If the message is on faith, then the skit deals with faith. The short scenes are comedic and contain a message I ping-pong off and into my message.

When the drama ministry first started, eighth through eleventh graders participated in the skits. Some of them were good, but most were not mature enough. By using seniors and college-age kids in our drama team, the young people respond to them more. They are better developed in their skills, and our dramas really began to improve.

8. Give a skillful and persuasive altar call every week.

Even if you know every student in your youth group is saved, still give an altar call. You never know what teenagers might be going through. Some may have just blown it and are thinking they are not saved. You want to give them the opportunity to pray and help them learn how to receive forgiveness.

If you give an altar call every week, you are showing your kids you will always have an altar call. They will know this is an opportunity for their unsaved friends to become born again. It also sends a message to them that the youth group is about reaching lost teens. Although having a good time is great, seeing as many young people born again as possible is what the youth ministry is all about.

The apostle Paul was a persuasive preacher. He was skilled in his ability to win people to the Lord. King Agrippa said to him, "You almost persuaded me to become a Christian." (Acts 26:28.) You are persuasive when you are passionate about something, and spending an eternity in heaven rather than hell is something all youth ministers should be passionate about.

We encourage positive pressure for a public response. When we give an altar call, we first have the teens raise their hands, and then we have them stand up. After they stand up, the other kids cheer and clap. Everyone is behind their decision for Christ. Once they come to the altar, we have trained counselors who will take them aside to counsel with them and give them follow-up materials.

9. Make each service seamless in transition.

This simply means that you should go quickly from one part of the service to the next. Everyone should be trained to always be prepared. You do not want the musicians looking for their instruments or the actors looking for their costumes when they should be walking on stage. If you plan to show a video, your workers should have set up and tested the system long before it is time to hit the play button on the VCR. You never want to have awkward silent times when people are trying to get ready. This just says to kids that you did not take the time to prepare for them.

10. Challenge all ministry participants to continually improve their skills.

We are constantly encouraging our staff and volunteers to improve their skills regardless of the area in which they minister. It is easy to become complacent when you do something week after week. If you are continually striving to improve what you are doing, your ministry never becomes dry but is always fresh.

When you work to be the best at what you do, you will draw a crowd. People are naturally attracted to quality. When you hear disgruntled reports from other youth pastors, be quick to mend the bridge and encourage them in the fact that this is a team effort. I guarantee you, there are more than enough unsaved teenagers in your community to fill all of the churches in your area.

TOUGH QUESTIONS

Q: Our youth group's focus is discipleship not in trying to attract big crowds. Is that okay?

A: I don't think so. It is great to have an emphasis on discipleship, and to excel at that. Certainly there is nothing wrong with that being the hallmark of your ministry. But I believe it is important that you never do something at the expense of another important part of your ministry. You have to continue to focus on reaching out beyond your own youth group.

You really cannot disciple unless you have converts. You can only disciple and mentor kids so long before they grow out of your youth group, and then you will have to reach more kids. You have to strike a balance of reaching the lost and making sure you have good discipleship as well.

Q: It seems like you put a lot of emphasis on "numbers." Can you go too far?

A: Yes and no. Yes, you can go too far if you don't do the other things that are important in ministry—discipleship, ongoing ministry, missions, developing teams and small groups. If all you have is a crowd every Wednesday or Friday night and you really do not take it any further than that, then your only emphasis is numbers and you are in trouble.

On the other hand, you have to continue to go after numbers and desire to grow. There are numbers going to hell every day in your community. We are into numbers. Part of our vision is to reach huge numbers of students. But our emphasis on numbers is not to compete with the youth group down the street or the church down the road. We look at how many numbers are in the devil's kingdom or, if you will, Satan's youth group.

In addition, we want to excommunicate those kids out of the devil's youth group, into our youth group, and we want to get as many as we can. Our mission at Oneighty® is to make it hard for teenagers in Tulsa to go to hell.

If they want to go to hell from Tulsa, Oklahoma, they are going to have to work at it, and we are determined to make it hard. We have to have a heart for the lost. Jesus came to save sinners.

Q: With all the new music, drama, and video in the church today, are we becoming too entertainment-oriented?

A: You can be too entertainment-oriented only if the Word of God is taken out of what you are doing. It is important to be as relevant as we possibly can. Scripture teaches us that. Paul writes in 1 Corinthians 9:22 the importance of being all things to all men. Young people are an entertainment generation. They love music, movies, the Internet, and humor. You can take all the things that capture their attention and cause them to listen to your message.

If your message is lost in the entertainment, then you have definitely gone too far. If you have ever found your ministry to be void of preaching the Word of God, then you are doing too many other things.

We make sure the center of everything we do on Wednesday nights at Oneighty® is preaching the Word. If I have to throw anything out, it will not be the preaching. If we have to throw the drama out, abbreviate the worship, or not show a video that night, fine. But we will never eliminate the preaching of the Word because that is what Jesus uses to save people and give people faith.

Faith comes by hearing, and hearing by the Word of God, so we must continue to preach the Word.

rule six:

get radical, preach the gospel, and hope they get it

I have visited youth groups throughout the United States and have attended many youth rallies. Often when I listen to youth ministers speak, I hear their message filled with the latest spiritual lingo, every sentence laced with holy zingers, Christian cliches, and religious buzzwords.

However, 80 percent of their audience consists of middle-of-the-road, unchurched, or unsaved kids who just sit there. They do not have any idea what the ministers are saying. The youth pastors continue to talk over their heads because they hear a small group of Christian teens shouting, "Amen! Praise God!" They are encouraged by the feedback but do not realize they are alienating the majority of the young people.

The sixth rule is prevalent in the church today.

Rule Six: *Get radical, preach the gospel, and hope they get it.*

Unfortunately, most ministers do not think it is their responsibility to make the message clear. They believe it is up to the audience to pick up and understand what they are saying. They feel their sole responsibility is just to "preach the truth, brother." They do not have time to cater to immature or carnal Christians. After all, if they would spend some time reading their Bible, they would understand the message.

If a restaurant had that kind of attitude, it would lose business quickly. The owner would never think of throwing food into a trough and letting the customers pick through it. Presentation is everything. If customers do not like the way their food looks, it is not their problem. It is the owner's problem when they send their food back to the kitchen. The owner will lose business if adjustments are not made. The same holds true for your outreach.

Pastors justify their actions by saying, "I'm not going to compromise the Word to minister to teenagers." What they are really saying is they do not want to inconvenience themselves. It would be too much of a hassle for them to change their teaching methods. The bottom line is they do not really care if the young people get spiritual help or not. This attitude has to be replaced with the following truth.

Truth Six: *We have a spiritual mandate to proclaim the gospel in a way teenagers can understand.*

In the parable of the sower found in Matthew 13, the same seed fell on four different types of soil. Jesus compared the various types of ground to the way we hear and understand the Word of God. First, seed fell by the wayside. Birds devoured this seed. (v. 4.) Jesus compared it to people who do not understand the Word. Lack of understanding makes it easy for the devil to snatch it away. (v. 19.)

Second, some seed fell on stony ground. This soil was shallow and had no depth. (vv. 5,6.) This is compared to people in whom the Word does not have a firm root in their hearts. As soon as they experience persecution, they immediately stumble and fall away. (vv. 20,21.)

Third, seed fell among thorns and became choked. (v. 7.) In this example, people hear the Word; however, they are too caught up in the cares of the world. Instead of trusting in the Word, they are choked by their fears. Others are caught in the deceitfulness of riches. They are more concerned with the pleasures and glamour of money than about the Word of God. The Word, then, becomes unfruitful in their lives. (v. 22.)

Finally, seed fell on good ground. (v. 8.) The comparison is made to people who hear, understand, and act upon the Word. They receive a thirty, sixty, and hundredfold return on what they understand. (v. 23.) These results are based on how well they understand the Word they hear.

If you look at the three types of soil in which the Word did not become fruitful, you will see in two cases, unfruitfulness was the fault of the hearer. They gave up when they were persecuted. They also quit standing on the Word because of worldly cares or the deceitfulness of riches.

Let's take another look at the first soil that was mentioned. The devil easily stole this Word because they did not understand what they heard. (v. 19.) The fault, therefore, lies with the minister. He failed to deliver the Word in a way it could be understood. We need to accept the responsibility of how our audience understands our message. If they cannot understand us, we have to change our method of delivery.

The apostle Paul said he became all things to all people. He wanted to win as many people as possible to the Lord. (1 Cor. 9:19-23.) In order to do this, he would do whatever it took to relate to his audience. To the Jew, he became a Jew. To the weak, he became weak. His goal was a harvest of souls, and he did whatever it took to make his message understood.

Too Much Christian Jargon

All too often we use Christian clichés without any type of explanation to the visitors. We assume everyone knows what we are talking about. Most of your audience will know what you are saying, but a third of them will not. The unchurched and unsaved kids do not understand Christian lingo, and using it in the service will scare them off.

When unchurched new visitors come to a youth group and hear the minister shout at the top of his rather large lungs, "How many of you are washed in the blood?" they do not know what you are talking about. They have never heard this kind of terminology before. Take a moment to think about what is going through their minds: *What blood? Whose blood? How do you wash in blood? Do they take baths in blood here? This place is weird. I bet this is a cult! Maybe I better get out of here!*

Everyone has heard ministers who cannot speak without saying "Praise the Lord" or "Hallelujah" at every comma and at the end of each sentence. "Praise God, how many are here, hallelujah, for the first time, glory be to the most high God?"

The kids just sit there with blank looks on their faces thinking, Can't you be *like a normal human being and talk right?* All we are doing is reinforcing stereotypes in their minds: Christians are weird and do not have a firm grasp on reality. While we are pouring our hearts out to reach them, they do not understand a word we are saying.

Communicate to Teens

Proverbs 15:2 TLB says, "A good teacher makes learning a joy." We then have to assume a bad teacher makes learning a drag. Ministering to teenagers can be intimidating. If you are boring them with your message, they can make you feel totally inadequate just by the looks on their faces. However, getting the gospel message to them can be both clear and compelling, even entertaining at times. To make the process easier for you, I have listed nine steps that will aid in your communication to young people.

1. Learn how to craft a message in point form.

Good communicators always have points. If teenagers know you have a beginning, middle, and an end, they will stay with you. You will lose them if they think you will never end. You want to let them know you are making progress. If they know you have five points and after 15 minutes you are on your fourth point, all is good! However, if you are still on your first point after 93 minutes, they know they are in for a long night, if they are still there.

2.   Research and acquire the right information.

Carefully study the Scripture. Teenagers are smart. They can tell when you have thrown a message together. Make sure you set aside enough time for the study of the Word. There is no substitute for study, research, and preparation.

3.   Stay current with youth culture.

You can keep up with what is hot by becoming a casual observer of their entertainment. I do this by what I call the "4M Plan." I will look through their magazines, listen to their music, walk through the malls, and go to their movies. You will be more effective in your communication when you know something about what they are reading and watching on TV.

I also have several "culture consultants" in my church. They keep me abreast of what is going on. These high school and college students know everything that is current. I talk to them all the time, and they let me know what's hot. They are on top of the music scene and know who everyone is listening to, and they tell me about the movies they have seen. You do not have to go to all the movies—just talk to people who have. You will actually look like you know what you are talking about when you minister to your youth group by keeping up with what is current in the youth culture.

You can find out whatever you want to know about teenagers by just asking them. We frequently do surveys with our young people and their parents. I would encourage you to be bold enough to ask what they like and do not like about the youth program. To find out what they think, do anonymous surveys. They will let you know the areas you need to improve.

Once you have analyzed the results, make any needed adjustments to what you are doing. If you have a valid reason why you do not plan to make any changes, at least address the comments you received. It can be frustrating to young people when you ask their opinion only to ignore it.

Tap into the information you can receive from cultural experts. The magazine *Plugged In* is a great magazine. It gives you the latest reviews on music and movies.[1] Josh McDowell Ministries, located in Dallas, Texas, also has material on the youth culture.[2] Barna Research Group, Ltd., located in Ventura, California, is an excellent Christian research company that studies today's cultural trends. Take advantage of the years of research they have done, and learn from them.[3]

It is not necessary to absorb the culture; simply counter it. Do not feel as though you have to dress and speak like the kids you are ministering to. If you are ten or fifteen years older than they are, they will know you are trying to act like them. Just be you. You only need to know enough about the youth culture so you can speak to it.

4. Develop stories and illustrations to drive each point home.

Jesus was a master illustrator. Learn from His example. Your sermons need to be more than a spiritual point or a scriptural quote. You have to go beyond that and give practical illustrations about what you are teaching. In Matthew chapters 6 and 7, Jesus gave numerous illustrations about the spiritual truths He was talking about.

An Illustrated Sermon

When I talk about virginity and keeping yourself pure, I use a powerful illustration kids never forget. I hold up a can of Coke and ask, "Who wants a drink?" The can is passed around as several teenagers throughout the audience drink from the can. As each young person takes a drink, everyone knows more backwash is filling the can. I pass it around until there is only a small amount left.

I hold up the can and ask, "Who wants to polish off this Coke?" I usually get two or three junior high boys who want to gross everyone out by drinking the backwash. After the last kid downs it, to the groans of the entire audience, I bring out a brand new, cold can of Coke. It is nice and fresh and, more importantly, untouched. I tell the crowd, "All right. I am not going to share this with everyone. I am only going to give it to one person. Who wants to drink this whole can of Coke?"

All the teens start screaming and yelling because they want the untouched soda. I then invite one of the teens on stage and ask them to drink the entire soda while everyone watches. Then I tell them, "When you save yourself for marriage, you are like this fresh can of Coke on your marriage night. You have not been opened. You are not full of spiritual, physical, and emotional backwash. You have not been passed around and shared with every guy or girl. You have saved yourself for your husband or wife."

Then I ask them, "How many of you want to be a fresh can of Coke? Who wants to be a can filled with backwash?" Everyone wants to be the fresh can of soda. They leave understanding the power of purity and why we keep our virginity until we are married. Many of the young people will not remember the Scripture I use with that illustration, 1 Corinthians 6:18, which simply says, "Flee fornication," but they will remember that can of coke.

5. Use humor to sustain attention.

Humor is just over-exaggeration. It is always a good icebreaker, as long as it is not overdone. When kids laugh at you, they are really saying they like you or they like what they are hearing.

All our drama skits are comedic. We rarely do anything with heavy drama. Humor also breaks the stereotype that church is always serious. In some churches it would be considered irreverent to laugh and have a good time. We use comedy to make a point. It is guaranteed that teenagers will remember what is said when it is wrapped in humor.

6. Use voice inflection and eye contact.

Part of being a good communicator is being a good storyteller. With that comes voice inflection. Learn how to use your voice to make a point in your message. Speaking softly can be just as effective, if not more effective, in illustrating a point. Other times, a loud, booming voice will drive the point home.

When you minister, look the young people right in the eye. Direct eye contact means different things. To the teenager trying to act tough, eye contact lets him know you are not intimidated. On the other hand, eye contact to some teenagers lets them know you care. You give the message that they are important when you look them directly in the eye.

7. Enforce discipline when behavior is disruptive.

Protect the right of every student to hear. We do not allow disruptive teens to dominate meetings. Adult ushers are in place to strictly enforce our rules.

8. Always bring each message to a point of commitment.

I always give an altar call at the end of every service. (Altar calls are covered in detail in Chapter 7.)

9. Preach for as long as you can hold their attention.

The attention span of teenagers usually lasts for twenty to thirty minutes. Interestingly enough, it is the length of most of their television programs. However, if you can only preach for fifteen minutes without losing their attention, do not go twenty. Find something else to do with the other five minutes. It is better to have ended your sermon while you have their attention, than to go five more minutes to make a point. If you lose them in the last minute, they will only remember that they thought you would never stop.

Preparing a sermon in a way that teenagers will listen and understand is not difficult. If you feel as though your words fall to the ground after you speak them, follow the example of Jesus and become an illustrated storyteller. While the presentation may not be a traditional method of preaching, a story will stay a long time in the hearts and minds of your young people.

TOUGH QUESTIONS

Q: Blaine, teenagers simply scare me. How can I speak to them with confidence?

A: They scare everyone. We had a pastor of one of the largest churches in America, who is also a well-known television minister, tell us he has preached to crowds of 10, 15, and 20 thousand people without fear. He said, "You put me before 50 teenagers, and I'm scared out of my mind."

They are intimidating as a group. If you want to grow in your confidence, there are a couple things you should do.

Number one, you have to spend time praying and hearing from God. The Lord told Jeremiah as he was seeking God, "Do not be afraid of their faces. You go where I tell you to go, speak what I tell you to speak." When you get with God, He gives you a boldness you cannot find on your own. He will give you a desire and strength as you stand before those kids, and a message they need to hear.

Number two, I have found it is best to keep working on it, and as you grow in experience, your confidence will grow.

Number three, look beyond those sometimes hard faces, or cold stares, into the hearts of young people and see their needs.

Some of these kids come from broken homes. They are insecure and have serious issues. If you can look toward their needs to see what they need, that will help you respond with compassion and the courage to say, "Hey, this is what God has for you." Look beyond your fears, and let God give you a love, compassion, and boldness as you speak each week to your kids.

Q: Where do you get your illustrations, statistics, quotes, and other message resources?

A: I am an avid collector. I encourage you to take the time when you come across something that is interesting, to file it, write it down, or clip it out. I read the newspaper almost every day, and I clip out articles and surveys, and file them for a future message. Do the same thing with the magazines you read. Things you see on the Internet, download them, print them, and put them in a file. Mark up books you read with yellow marker, and photocopy things you see that you can use for future messages. Take things that really ring strong with you that you hear from other ministers and write them down. Be a good collector.

Q: How do you choose the right topics to speak about to your group?

A: There are three things I do. First, I pray and listen to God. I say, *"Lord, what would You have me share in the next week or month with our kids?"* I usually preach in series, so I might spend two to four weeks on one subject. I sense in prayer that the Lord wants me to share a certain area with our kids.

Second, when I am in church on weekends and sitting under my pastor's ministry, I hear him preach. Many times I think, *Our kids need to hear this. I want to reemphasize this in our youth ministry.* I take cues from my pastor and realize what he is teaching our church isn't just for the adults, but for the kids as well. It is important to disseminate that and make it relevant to our young people.

Third, realize there are certain things every year I believe your kids need to hear, especially as you get new kids into your ministry. They need to hear how to have good relationships with each other, how to respect authority, how to receive forgiveness for sin, and how to repent. Those things need to be an annual part of your preaching repertoire.

rule seven:

refuse to compromise by using food, games, or facilities to draw teenagers to church

Architects have spent countless hours designing magnificent church buildings with high cathedral ceilings and stained glass windows. Their goal was to design buildings that would attract people to worship God. However, to today's teenagers, the facility is irrelevant and unappealing.

In order to combat a "churchy" stereotype, we gave our facility an "image makeover" by removing all religious trappings from our building. We do not have doves hanging from the ceiling, nor do we have a cross on the stage. Do we believe in the Cross and the Holy Spirit? You bet. We preach on both.

Our style has developed to a point where anyone who visits Oneighty® will never associate us with traditional church. The kids love our facility! When they see the game room, café, and auditorium, they think, **Man, this place is great!** Our philosophy, however, completely goes against the seventh rule.

Rule Seven: *Refuse to compromise by using food, games, or facilities to draw teenagers to church.*

I have had many people ask me if I felt like I have gone overboard on our facility. The answer is no. George Bernard Shaw once wrote, "The reasonable man adapts himself to the world: the unreasonable one persists in trying to adapt the world to himself. Therefore, all progress depends on the unreasonable man."[1]

We are now in the seventh millennium since the creation of Adam. Unreasonable relevance is the order of the day for the millennium seven youth ministry. If there is one thing the church has not been, it is relevant to teenagers. Most churches preach the Word, but many of those churches are not packaging their message in a manner in which teens can relate.

Some pastors would never dream of setting up a café in their youth facility. It is outside their traditional thinking. The thought of putting arcade games on church property is enough to make others call the notion ungodly. However, if we want to reach our young people, Rule Seven needs to be replaced with the following truth.

Truth Seven: *As fishers of men, God will give us wisdom on where and how to catch fish.*

Depending on the type of fish you want to catch depends on the type of bait and equipment you use. Deep-sea fishermen use different bait than those who are in the mountains fishing for trout. Commercial fishermen use large nets to catch tuna, while you and I would typically use a rod and reel in our favorite fishing spot. What is important is that you use the right method of fishing for the type of fish you want to catch. In the same way, God will show us the best way to "catch" many kids.

Using Ambiance to Draw Kids

If you want to draw teenagers to your facility, you have to create an environment that will attract them. Keep in mind that the atmosphere plays an important role in whether or not they return.

Unlike the animal kingdom, God created mankind to enjoy ambiance. Animals do not care where they eat. Take for instance farm animals. You can feed cows hay inside or outside the barn. They will eat off the ground with just as much ease as from a food trough. They don't care where they eat; they just want to eat.

On the other hand, people are very concerned about their environment. We were created to desire an appealing environment. That is why we will pay twenty dollars at a steakhouse for a three-dollar piece of meat. We pay for atmosphere. We like to hear soft music while we dine by candlelight. Good restaurants work just as hard to create attractive surroundings as they do excellent food.

Where to Start

When we started Oneighty®, we were far from where we are today. While we have made many changes over the years, we are a long way from where we want to go.

Youth pastors who visit our facility wonder how and where they should begin in turning their facility into a cool-looking youth center. My advice is always the same. You can only start where you are and with the resources available to you.

When Pastor George decided to start the youth program, long before we started Oneighty®, Church On The Move was meeting In a hotel. At the time, one hundred people attended the church. Fifteen of them were teenagers. The only available space the church had for the youth program was in the ministry warehouse. The space was not the best, but we put a lot of effort into making it a unique youth facility.

We stacked up boxes to create our stage area. Then we put different colored lights behind the boxes. Since the ceiling was about thirty feet high, we dropped a parachute over our meeting area to make a roof-like covering. We shot colored lights through the white parachute. Our sound system was small but decent. Finally, to add a little pizzazz to the room, we set up the chairs in a unique pattern.

We did the very best with what we had. Amazingly, the kids thought it was great! The parachute intrigued some of the first-time visitors. They would point to the ceiling and ask, "What's the deal with that?" Everyone thought I was into skydiving. None of our kids knew why it was there; they just thought it was cool.

I came to realize that to a teenager "cool" is anything that does not have a purpose. If it should not be there, it is cool. We, therefore, started to put stuff in our facility that did not have any purpose whatsoever.

Have you ever noticed many of the popular restaurants today have old bicycles, wagons, and other paraphernalia attached to their walls and ceilings? It's cool, because it has no purpose and should not be there.

When Oneighty® began, we did not have any games, nor did we serve food. Over the years we have slowly grown and evolved. Pastors ask me if we had a master plan to get where we are today. We did not. We had only a one-month plan. Now we put more effort into our strategy and have projected goals for the year, but not much further than that. Just trying to keep up with what God has given us to do every day keeps us busy enough.

The Outward Appearance

The parachute has long been removed. Today when you enter the facility, the first thing you see is our logo. It does not have a hint of religion to it. Then, in the auditorium, you will notice the restrooms. We have a picture of James Dean pointing to the boys' restroom and another of Marilyn Monroe pointing to the girls' restroom. Our hallways are decorated with life-size images of Superman and other entertainment icons.

We once had a youth pastor visit the facility who informed me that we put far too much emphasis on the physical—on our facility and image. He even quoted Scripture: "For man looketh on the outward appearance, but the Lord looketh on the heart" (1 Sam. 16:7). That Scripture, however, only confirms everything I have been saying. We are not trying to reach God. We are trying to reach young men and women. Since they are concerned about appearances, we have to pay attention to them as well.

When we look at the instructions God gave Moses for the building of the temple, we see that He is concerned about ambiance. When Solomon built a temple for the Lord, it was so magnificent that the Queen of Sheba fainted when she saw it. (1 Kings 10:4,5.) If we would try to reproduce Solomon's temple today, the cost would run in the billions. God looks at the condition of your heart, but He also uses the outward appearance to draw people to Himself. Then He can reach their hearts.

Today's youth are more image-conscious than any other generation. In fact, the only thing important to them is image. Look at the clothes they wear, the things they buy, and the way they talk. It all fits the image they want to project.

What we are really dealing with is a bunch of carnal kids. This does not mean we should leave our Bibles at home and do music shows and juggling acts every week. You have to put some thought behind how to effectively get the gospel message to them. If you fail to reach them on the image level first, you will never be able to touch their heart or spirit.

Thirteen Keys to a Magnetic Youth Facility

To help you create a dynamic facility, here are thirteen steps you can use to dramatically change your current space.

1. Use colors wisely.

Do not allow institutional colors to dominate your youth room. That means no beige walls or gray chairs. If you have gray chairs, paint them. If your walls are beige, put something on them. It should not look like a hospital or a schoolroom. Do everything you can to give the facility some color.

A great place to go for ideas is the local mall. Take some of your core young people with you to show you stores they like. Look at the store design. They have spent a lot of money to find out what attracts young people. Use their style as a springboard to get ideas on what to do with your space.

2. Shoot out all of your fluorescent lights.

At least turn them off. We use inexpensive warehouse lights that can be dimmed. This type of lighting is a lot more attractive than bright, fluorescent lighting.

Pay attention to stage lighting. Sometimes during worship we dim the stage lights. When the speaker gets ready to preach, we turn on the high intensity lights to draw everyone's attention to the stage.

3. Make your logo and name prominent.

I recommend developing a non-religious name. Many youth groups have churchy, religious names. If the name of your youth group is "Kids Who Love God" or "First Pentecostal Christian Youth Ministry International," change it! Thank God for your church name and for the fact that your teenagers love the Lord. Names like that, however, do not attract unchurched kids.

Instead, come up with a name that has spiritual significance but does not sound religious. Oneighty® is extremely spiritual to us. It means repentance and turning. An individual was going one way and decided to turn around and go the other way. Without quoting any Scripture, the name has powerful meaning. When teenagers see the name for the first time, I am sure they do not think of repentance. It might invoke thoughts of skateboarding but certainly nothing religious.

Years ago leaders from the national office of the Foursquare Church movement came to see what Oneighty® was all about. They fell in love with the principles and methods that made Oneighty® work and went back and developed their own national name and program. They call it "U-Turn," and they are having tremendous success. The way their logo is designed does not lead you to believe U-Turn is a church youth group. Most unchurched teens do not have any idea of its biblical reference.

It would be important to add here that the Oneighty® and U-Turn logos are trademarked and protected nationally. Please do not use these names and logos in your church without official permission through ministry affiliation. We conduct one-day seminars for pastors on how to turn their youth ministry around. At the end of each seminar, we give an affiliation application to any pastor interested in using the Oneighty® name and logo and, more importantly, the principles that make it work.

Today we have more than 100 Gold affiliate churches and another 250 Silver affiliates. We protect our name because we have worked hard to build its reputation for youth ministry excellence. Moreover, it would be confusing for teenagers to hear about multiple Oneighty® programs in the same city.

3. Show the vision with pictures.

Youth programs are about teenagers. They love to look at other young people. When you look at print advertising directed toward teenagers, you will see pictures of young people doing fun things. This appeals to teens. We piggybacked their idea and had pictures taken of our kids having fun and hanging out together. We sent the photos off for enlargement, had them laminated for protection, and hung them on walls throughout our facility.

4. Create as much sound as possible.

Today's young people like a lot of sound—the louder the better. Some of our adult workers scream because we turn it up so loud, including my own mom and dad, but kids like it loud.

5. Drop banners from high ceilings.

An inexpensive way to fill in the empty space of high ceilings is to use banners. We screen-printed our logo on burlap banners. You can use any type of material you want.

6. Put up burlap sound baffles in large rooms.

Sound baffles filled with fiberglass will help deaden sound in large rooms. They work especially well if you have high ceilings. Once you install them you will notice a marked improvement in your sound.

7.   Create a free game area to be used before and after meetings.

All our games are free. If you prefer, you can lease coin-operated games. We wanted to be one up on the local arcade, so ours are free. More importantly, we want every student who comes to be able to play games.

We look for arcade games that are at least two years old and buy them used. By doing this you can usually get a used machine for half the price of a new one. If you decide to purchase pinball machines, understand that they will require regular maintenance. If you have several machines, you can expect to have a maintenance man out about once a month. There are so many little gadgets in a pinball machine that something always needs to be adjusted. Maintenance is very important. The last thing you want is a room full of kids with half your games out of order.

Some of the maintenance-free games are Nintendo, Play Station, billiards, and pool. We had many of the eight balls stolen from our pool tables, so we eventually posted an adult to monitor the poolroom at all times. The kids now have to check the pool balls in and out.

8.   Have a DJ in the sound booth before and after meetings.

I recommend setting up a sound booth where a DJ can play music, make announcements, and call out kids' names when their parents arrive to pick them up. We also have a DJ set up on one side of the stage in our service auditorium. He plays music as the kids come in and leave.

9.   Build a unique pulpit.

There are different things you can do to create a great pulpit design. We welded a bunch of transmission gears together to make ours. A simple idea for a pulpit is to get an old oil barrel and paint your logo on it. If you are stuck on ideas, hold a brainstorming session to develop a theme that will be relevant for your kids.

10. Use steel grating over part of your stage.

By using steel grating, you can put your monitors underneath the platform. This will free up space on your stage. You will still be able to hear the sound, but the monitors won't be in your way. We also put lights and a smoke machine underneath our stage for special effects.

11. Develop a food service area.

Food is a great way to draw teenagers to your youth group. They like to hang out and eat. We sell our food for what it costs us. That way, anyone who comes can buy some-thing to eat. Many times during a special event, we give our food away. Some minis-ters tell me when I do that, I am using food to bribe young people. My response is, "Bribery is an inducement to commit an illegal act." There is nothing wrong when teenagers use free food as an incentive to get their friends to come to church. What is illegal about attending a youth service?

Jesus was concerned about food. Twice He had the opportunity to send multitudes away to find their own food. Instead, He took the time to feed a multitude of five thousand people. Later, He fed another four thousand men, women, and children. (Matt. 14:15-21; Mark 8:1-9.)

Food has often been used as a way to draw people to an event. When the publicans and sinners came to Matthew's "all-you-can-eat" feast, they did not come to hear Jesus preach. (Luke 5:29.) I guarantee you they came to eat. They may have heard some guy named Jesus was going to be there, but scrumptious food at a rich tax collector's house was the drawing point.

The first incident of strife in the early church was over a lack of food. (Acts 6:1.) Widows were not being fed their daily portion of food. The disciples did not ignore the problem or say it was unimportant. They took care of the situation by appointing seven deacons to handle food service.

When we first started to serve food at Oneighty®, we did not make any of it ourselves. Originally, we made arrangements with McDonald's or Taco Bueno. We would order three hundred hamburgers or burritos at a time. Since we were ordering in such large quantities, we were able to get a good discount for the food. We timed it so the food would arrive at the Oneighty® center as the service let out.

We have never used food as a way to make money. It has always been one of the many tools we use to attract young people.

12. Properly staff and supervise each area of the facility.

When we first opened the game room, it was not staffed properly. We had kids who would push a student off a game because they wanted to play it. Monitors were immediately stationed in the room to make sure nothing got out of hand. We also had parents who would come through the game room to pick up their kids after the service. Sometimes they could not find them, nor could they find a staff member who knew what was going on.

Consequently, we installed "game room monitors" in every area of the facility. They are properly identified with the same colored shirt and name tags. Parents feel more at ease dropping off their children because they realize we have everything under control.

Creating a youth facility that will attract young people is not as hard you think. Oneighty® has an old town/industrial theme, which works well for our area. While this may not work in other parts of the country, you can take the principles outlined in this chapter to create a facility that will be relevant to the young people in your community.

TOUGH QUESTIONS

Q: We are reaching many students without using "cool" facilities or games. Are you sure this stuff is for everyone?

A: If you are reaching a lot of kids without using any games or a cool-looking facility, then I have to commend you. You are doing a great job and are obviously doing it with the ability you have developed to communicate well. You have probably formed a good team of leaders.

How many more kids would you be reaching if you worked on your facilities, added games, and put food into the mix? Don't feel like any of those things are compromising because they are fun things or things that appeal more to the social needs of kids. Realize that with these extra things you will probably do even better and reach more kids, and isn't that our goal?

Paul said, "I will do all things to all men, that I might be able to save some" (1 Cor. 9:22). He said he would use every method possible to reach as many people as he could. Don't be satisfied with where you are; be grateful, but move forward.

Q: Won't the use of carnal things like games, food, etc. attract a bunch of carnal kids?

A: Sure it will. Don't you want to reach the carnal kids? Don't you want to bring those kids in and give them a chance to grow in their walk with God and maybe move into a more spiritual Christianity? Certainly there will be some kids who initially come only for the games, food, fun, or to meet their friends.

If you're preaching and discipling well, and your services are full of the Holy Spirit and done in a way that inspire and convict, you're going to see changes in those kids. They will move out of their carnal habits into spiritual habits.

We hope to draw many carnal kids. We want kids who don't even know Christ, and if they come initially for some of the more social reasons, wonderful, but they won't stay that way for long.

We found as we developed these methods that we have more spiritual kids than we have ever had. We have more kids going on mission trips, attending discipleship, and reaching their schools for Christ than ever before. These have not hindered our spiritual kids. It is emboldening them to reach more of their friends and use these tools to help bring them in.

Q: All this stuff costs money, which is something we don't have much of. Any suggestions?

A: Sure, the first thing would be to work with what you have, and start small. Again, it all goes back to one Scripture. Jesus said if you are faithful in the little, He will make you ruler over much. If you have only fifty dollars a month in your budget right now, do the best you can with that budget. Be faithful with it, put your heart and soul into that ministry, and God will continue to give you more.

Proclaim your vision. As you share your vision with people and have a heart for what you are doing, God will give you provision. Provision always follows vision.

Believe God. The Bible says in Mark 11:24 that whatsoever things you desire, pray for those things and believe you'll receive them, and you'll have them. You are not limited to your church budget. God can use other sources to bring you the finances you need.

God cares about your ministry, and if you will pray and trust Him, He will provide for you.

rule eight:

never borrow someone's ideas when you can easily
come up with worse ones on your own

I often hear youth ministers say they would never use someone else's idea. They want to be original and would never copy another ministry. Although they may try to be completely original, they cannot. No one ever is. Never using an idea because it did not come directly from God will only hinder your ministry. This type of attitude religiously follows the eighth rule.

Rule Eight: *Never borrow someone's ideas when you can easily come up with worse ones on your own.*

God wants us to share our resources. The principle of giving and receiving is found throughout the Bible and applies to more than money. When sharing ideas, the person who uses someone else's idea is blessed. He did not have to spend a lot of wasted time trying to find out what works and what does not. The person who shared his idea is also blessed because he will receive back more in return. Many times by sharing an idea, we will spark a better idea. This principle follows the truth that replaces Rule Eight.

Truth Eight: *God gives His people proven transferable models, patterns, and ideas to reproduce and imitate.*

We are encouraged to imitate successful Christian leadership. The apostle Paul told the church of Corinth to pattern themselves after him. (1 Cor. 11:1.) Jesus said in the book of John that by entering the labor of others you would reap from their labor. (John 4:37,38.) Paul later commended the Thessalonians because as they copied him, they then became an example to believers in Macedonia and Achaia. (1 Thess. 1:6,7.)

This is a principle God wants us to follow. I encourage you to look for models that are successful in other ministries. As you copy those models into your own ministry, you will also achieve success.

Sharing Ideas

One of the exciting things about the Oneighty® affiliate network is we not only share ideas, but receive ideas from our affiliates as well. I received a great idea from one of our affiliates in Roswell, Texas. Their Oneighty® program had quickly grown to several hundred kids. However, teenagers who did drugs, as well as local drug dealers, started to come to their youth program. They soon had students trying to smoke and do drugs while visiting their youth facilities.

They wanted to reach these kids but, at the same time, wanted them to respect their rules and facilities. They contacted the police and asked for advice. The police suggested they bring their drug-sniffing dogs to the next meeting.

When the pastor got up that night to take the offering, he said, "We are going to take two offerings tonight. First, we are going to receive your offering of cash donations. Then, we are going to receive another offering. Tonight would be a good night to put any drugs you have in your possession in that offering. Right after we take up the collection, we are going to send drug-sniffing dogs down the aisles. They will sniff out any drugs you thought you could hide. If the dogs smell drugs on you, you will be taken to the local jail and charged with the possession of an illegal substance. We encourage you to give generously tonight!" After they collected the offering buckets, they found them filled with all kinds of drugs, pipes, and joints. Some kids even threw in their cigarettes!

We plan to use this idea sometime, although we do not have a big problem with drugs. Anytime we catch students with drugs we have them arrested and meet with their parents. You cannot play with situations like that, and you have to let the kids know you are serious. We will pray with them on their way to jail, as the police are leading them out the door. Anytime we have criminal activity at Oneighty®, whether it is a gang fight, drugs, or vandalism, we prosecute immediately. Therefore, we do not have many problems in this area.

Seven Keys to Implementing Models and Ideas

There are many good models being used by successful youth ministries. As you sift through the different programs, you will find ideas and strategies that work perfect for your own ministry. Bringing new ideas into your church can sometimes prove challenging. Listed below are guidelines you can follow to aid in the implementation of any new program.

1. Be thoroughly convinced the model or idea has a scriptural foundation.

We believe everything we do is based on the Word. You should not do something solely because it worked for another ministry. There must be a scriptural foundation for everything you do and any change you make. Let me give you an example.

We have been criticized for rewarding students for bringing friends by giving them something special for their efforts. The principle of work and reward is shown throughout the Bible. We are rewarded with blessings for giving. (Luke 6:38.) Children are rewarded with a good, long life for obeying their parents. (Eph 6:1.)

Maybe you remember David's comments about fighting Goliath. The brash teenager exclaimed, "What shall be given to the man who slays this Philistine?" He found out he would get the king's daughter's hand in marriage, a chunk of the king's cash, and no more taxes! He quickly took care of the giant. Did David love God? Yes. Did David want the rewards? Sure.

I believe our young people can serve God with a pure heart and be rewarded for doing so at the same time. The point is, know that all you are doing is supported by the principles of the Word of God.

2. Add your own unique flavor to anything you borrow.

Take what you borrow and make it something that will work for you. Not long ago we had some youth ministers from New York City visit Oneighty®. They had a church in the Bronx. After they walked through our facility, they said, "Blaine, none of this would appeal to our kids. They are not into old-time, western, antique looking stuff. This works for you in Oklahoma, but it won't work for us in the Bronx." I told them to use our program but find a different theme. Our program does not work because our facility has a western look to it. The Oneighty® model will work regardless of the setting. Just create a theme that will be relevant for your kids.

3. Translate ideas and models into your church, culture, and community.

We have various life-size entertainment icons on our walls. They work for us. You might work in a conservative church, and if you tried to put any type of icon on the wall, you would be excommunicated. If an idea could cause you to lose church members or your job, then do not do it. You can only do whatever works within your church culture and community. If you want to try something new, push the envelope as far as you can go, then stop.

Sometimes I have stretched a little too far, and I have had to make adjustments. Pastor George has had to reel me in from time to time. Flow with your pastor and church. If you cannot put up James Dean or Elvis, try Charlie Chaplin or whatever characters would be suitable for your church.

4. Sell changes and new ideas properly.

It is easy to get excited and immediately want to implement radical change. For some people, however, you have to slowly bring them around to a new view—especially your pastor.

He has to back any change you want to implement. If you now want to use a smoke machine and play your music louder than you have ever done before, explain to your pastor why this is beneficial to reaching young people. Once he is on board with the idea, he will back you when an irate parent runs to him complaining about the noise and smoke. Your pastor can help calm their fears by explaining you are not compromising the gospel message. Instead, you are fishing for souls.

Never announce a major change to your youth group without first talking to your leaders. They need to be kept on the inside track. A new idea to reach the unsaved kids in your community may sound carnal to your spiritual teens. If they question your plans, leaders can explain to them what you want to do. However, if they do not know what is going on, you will probably end up with two people against you.

5. Respond pro-actively to criticism.

Anytime you begin to grow you will be criticized. I have probably gotten more criticism in the last five years than any other time in my ministry. Yet at the same time, I have had more results with teenagers.

I have received legitimate criticism and saw I had to make changes. I have also had criticism that was not legitimate. The arcade games and our free food nights have been a major source of criticism. However, I have scriptural precedent for what we are doing, and the results can be seen in the changed lives of young people. This is criticism I have to live with.

I also get untruthful criticism. Sometimes people have trouble rejoicing over someone else's growth. They make up things and spread gossip just because they do not like your success. If I find the source of someone who is spreading rumors about Oneighty®, I contact him or her and address the issue.

Criticism is a part of growing, and you have to learn how to handle it. The Holy Spirit will show you how to deal with each situation. I have determined not to be a person who criticizes. As you rejoice in what the Lord is doing in your ministry, I will rejoice right beside you.

6. Don't allow the excuse of size or funding constraints paralyze you.

When visiting a large organization, you can leave overwhelmed or you can go away inspired. Remember that anything big always started small.

I visited a Nike Town in San Francisco. It is an amazing store. As I went through it, I thought of a book I read about Phil Knight, the founder. He started out with nothing. He was originally going to call his shoes "Dimension 6." An employee came up with the name Nike. It means goddess of victory. He thought it would be a good name since everyone in sports wants to be victorious.

Phil Knight, however, did not like it. He used the name only because it was shorter and would save money when putting it on the shoes. He asked an art student to develop a logo, and the swoosh was designed for thirty-five dollars.

He started out by selling the shoes out of the trunk of his car. He went to athletic dorms at different university campuses. As students came out of the dorm, he would try to sell them his shoes. Once the shoes were in the hands of star athletes, other athletes wanted to buy them too. We know the rest of the story.

Don't be discouraged by lack of money. Many successful companies started out the same way. Learn from their small beginnings and realize that with each step you take, you are one step closer to your goal.

7. Learn how to raise money for new projects.

Deuteronomy 8:18 says, "But thou shalt remember the Lord thy God: for it is he that giveth thee power to get wealth." The word power can also be translated **ability.** This Scripture does not say God will give you money; He will give you the ability to get money and create wealth. Whether you realize it or not, you have the ability to create wealth for your youth ministry.

In Malachi we are told tithing will cause God to open the windows of heaven and pour out blessings. (Mal. 5:10.) Some people think He will rain cash from heaven, but that never happens. What is it then that God pours out? Ingenious ideas! If you will act on these ideas, you will see financial blessings come into your life and ministry.

Raising Finances

God has given us some ingenious ideas. They are simple but have helped us raise money for different projects.

1. Pray.

It sounds easy, but it works. We have prayed for things and seen immediate answers.

We told a pastor who was visiting the facility about our visitor incentive program. After he saw the Oneighty® Mobile, he wanted a car for his youth group and prayed a short prayer. (More information about the Oneighty® Mobile can be found in Chapter 11.)

By the time he got back to the hotel that afternoon, his message light was blinking on the telephone. His secretary had left a message asking him to call. When he spoke to her, she told him a woman came to the church and dropped off keys to an old Corvette that had been sitting in her garage. It was in perfect working order. The woman said the Holy Spirit told her to give the car to the church. The secretary was sure the church did not need a Corvette and called the pastor to see how she should handle the situation. Of course, the pastor said, "Yes, we want the car!"

It would be nice if the answers to our prayers manifested that quickly! They don't always, but prayer does work. If you will pray for the things you need in your youth ministry, God will speak to the hearts of people to help you.

2. Promote your vision.

If you want to raise finances, you have to enthusiastically talk about what you are doing. This is not to manipulate people, but to let them know how they can get involved. We regularly hold banquets and invite people to hear about our goals and any immediate projects coming up.

3. Hold a basketball game between the church staff and the youth group.

This has become a popular event for us. We hold an annual basketball game shortly after the Final Four. We rent a high school gym and sell tickets. We also set up a concession stand and bring in more money through food sales. It is a fun game with lots of fellowship and entertainment. We have a lot of competition between the staff and the kids. It has been a great moneymaking machine for our mission program.

4. Sell Mother's Day roses.

This was an ingenious idea that came from heaven. My sister owns a flower shop. One day I asked her how much she pays for a rose. I was surprised when she told me thirty-nine cents. I immediately got the idea to sell roses to fathers as they are walking out of the church on Mother's Day. We ordered fifteen hundred roses, and my sister charged us fifty cents a rose.

We turned around and sold a single rose for $3.00, six roses for $6.95, and a dozen roses for $14.95. We set up tables at every exit. The first year we sold all the roses by the end of the second service. There was not a man in the building who could walk out the door without buying his wife or mother a rose. He would have to be heartless to do that! We now do this fundraiser every year.

I would suggest contacting the owner of a local flower shop. Share the vision of the youth ministry and the project you are undertaking. If you explain that this is a Mother's Day fundraiser, I am sure you will find an owner who is willing to work with you.

We also do a Father's Day bake sale from time to time. Our teenagers bring pies, cookies, candy, and cakes. We sell the desserts as inexpensively as possible. Again, no one wants to walk out of the church on Father's Day without getting dad a dessert.

5. Solicit business sponsorships.

We held an event several years ago called "Global TV." We brought in the Newsboys, and eight thousand young people filled the Oral Roberts University Mabee Center.

When we put our budget together, we realized everything was paid for except the advertising. That amounted to thirty thousand dollars. We came up with the idea of getting business sponsors to pay for our advertising.

We broke down each area of advertising and looked for businesses that would sponsor the different avenues of advertising. For their sponsorship, we promoted their business at Global TV. For example, the cost to print our posters was $5,000. We initially asked businesses to underwrite the entire amount. If they were unwilling to do that, we had different levels of sponsorship in which they could get involved. For the posters, we found two businesses that would pay $2,500 each. In turn, we put their logos on all the posters and in the programs we gave to the kids.

We determined how many sponsors we needed for each area of advertising and kept making telephone calls until everything was covered. You have to be willing to suffer a little rejection. We may have approached ten sponsors before we found two that would underwrite an area. At times we personally visited a business, but most of our contact was made by telephone or fax.

The different levels of sponsorship were called Gold, Silver, and Bronze. Of course, the Gold Level donated the most money. Their name was printed on every piece of advertising. The Silver Level had their name printed in the program as well as on the particular area they sponsored. The Bronze Level had their name printed only on the area they sponsored. You can also add incentives like tickets to the event, VIP seating, etc.

We sought out Christian business owners who believed in our cause. We advertised in our church bulletin and looked through the Yellow Pages. We looked for the Christian fish sign in any advertisement. We did get some sponsorships from secular businesses; however, these businesses were usually associated with our youth workers in some way. The sponsorships mainly came from Christian businesses.

As you move to a new level in your youth ministry, remember God is leading you each step of the way. Learn to break down your long-term goal into manageable steps. Always remember the importance of gaining the support of your pastor and leaders. Together you can implement new ideas that may go against the traditional thinking of church members.

TOUGH QUESTIONS

Q: Why don't you let any church use the name Oneighty® for their youth group?

A: When we first began to use the name Oneighty®, we did. We began to have churches use the name, but they did not put a lot of quality into their ministry. As we began to grow nationally and became known as a ministry, churches were not using the name in a quality way. It began to hurt our reputation. We had already trademarked the name, but we also began to protect the name.

The Lord dealt with us about helping churches that wanted to make an investment to use the name. We decided to develop a program that would help them do that. It is called our Oneighty® affiliation program. Every few months we bring in senior pastors who want to come in for a one-day training program. At the end of the day, they see Oneighty®. If they are interested in applying to be an Oneighty® affiliate, they go through the steps of the application. Then we check a number of things to make sure they qualify, such as to see if we're on the same page doctrinally, and if they are willing to make the same commitment we've made in terms of finances and resources. We want the pastor to be committed to the program. If all those things check out and we don't have an affiliate in that area, we will license them and allow them to use the name.

The Bible says a good name is better that riches; therefore, the goal of Oneighty® is to strive for an image of excellence throughout America. We are doing national programming, in some cases national television, and we want to make sure when the name Oneighty® is used, it is used with excellence, honor, and integrity; therefore, we must protect it.

Q: What do you do when parents in your church become critical of your methods of ministry?

A: Because we're always on the cutting edge of using new methods and developing different things that will work in reaching kids, we receive criticism. I have found it is best to respond to these parents. Remember, if you hear a criticism, be proactive and make a phone call to that parent. If a parent calls or writes a letter and is upset about something, or questions you in a certain area, set up an appointment to explain what you are doing. Nine times out of ten I have found that once they see your heart and why you do certain things, they will become a big supporter.

There may be some cases where a parent might help you see a problem you can change, or help you see another side of a problem you have not seen before. Build relationship bridges and don't make enemies. That doesn't mean you cower to every parent or give in to everything they ask for, but at least meet with them and help them see why you're doing what you're doing and try to win them over.

Q: Our ministry finances are fine, but personally, I'm struggling to pay my own bills. What should I do?

A: Trust God to meet your needs. He has promised to prosper you. Third John 2 says, "Beloved, I wish that you would prosper, and be in health, even as your soul prospers." God wants to prosper you to meet your needs, but you must take steps toward that as well. Be obedient in your giving and in your tithes; then allow God to speak to you and give you the steps to take to see prosperity come in your own life.

When I first started in the youth ministry, we struggled, and Cathy and I were not paying all the bills every month. I remember going to my pastor and saying, "What do I do? How can I grow here?" He gave me some encouragement and steps to take.

One of the steps was to seek God in prayer and allow the Lord to show me different ways He could open up new doors for me that would help meet our needs. We did that. I remember one month in December, Cathy and I prayed over the next year, and we said, "Lord, what can we do to grow in our finances this year?" The Lord gave me six or seven steps to take, and we did those steps. They were practical things we knew we needed to do, and as we got to the end of year, our finances had doubled.

God will give you steps to take in your own finances, and as you take those steps of obedience, your finances will grow. It starts with a spirit of faith and knowing that God wants to meet your needs. He will use many different sources to do that.

rule nine:

DO NOT FOCUS ON CARNAL THINGS LIKE NUMBERS AND ATTENDANCE

Some ministers feel it is not spiritual to focus on how many teenagers attend their services or how many new visitors come each week. They believe if they spend their time in the study of the Word and in prayer, the Holy Spirit will draw young people to their meetings. We have chosen to ignore this philosophy and break the ninth time-honored rule.

Rule Nine: *Do not focus on carnal things like numbers and attendance.*

All the ministry departments at Church On The Move focus on their attendance. In our outreach to young people, we believe we have a mandate to grow. In fact, if you look at the ministry of Jesus, you will notice He cursed the things He saw that were not growing.

In the book of Mark, we read about a time when Jesus and His disciples were leaving the city of Bethany. The Scripture notes that He was hungry. When He saw a fig tree, He expected to eat some fruit from it. However, the tree was barren, so He cursed it. (Mark 11:12-14.) In the "Parable of the Talents," the master took one talent from the unprofitable servant. He gave it to the servant with ten talents because he had multiplied what he was originally given. (Matt. 25:26-28.)

More than our bank accounts or material possessions, the one element God wants to see grow is the number of people added to His kingdom. Some pastors, however, are focused on their growth for competitive reasons. They want to have the largest church in their town. I believe if you do not have a compassion for the lost and a true love for people, your ministry will fizzle out in a year or two. Jesus had a genuine love for people, and that is where growth begins.

After the foundation of love is in place, there are practical skills you can learn in order to grow your attendance. They are found in Truth Nine.

Truth Nine: *God has given every church ministry the ability and the tools to experience growth and multiplication.*

I have been in leadership meetings where the minister gave an altar call for people to receive his anointing "to grow churches." You do not need hands laid on you for church growth. We all receive our anointing from the same place—the Spirit of God. You are no different from any other great man or woman of God.

God's Command To Grow

Church growth does not come from a special gift, and it is not a mystery. It is something anyone can accomplish if you will apply the Word of God and the principles found in this book to your situation.

From the very beginning, God commanded Adam and Eve to be fruitful and replenish the earth. (Gen. 1:28.) He placed within them the ability to multiply. This is evident as we look at our current world population of over six billion people. In His design of man, God gave the male reproductive system the ability to produce five hundred million sperm cells a day. You cannot tell me He does not know how to multiply things!

Not only does God multiply in the natural; He also multiplies souls for His kingdom. In Acts 2:41, it says, "There were **added** unto them about three thousand souls." Later in Acts 6, we see the number of disciples **multiplied** greatly. (v. 1.) How did the church go from addition to multiplication?

In Acts 2, Peter preached one message and gave one altar call. The result was the conversion of three thousand people. However, in the sixth chapter, we learn the disciples began to meet in various houses. Instead of one person, there were now between twelve and fifty ministers preaching the gospel, giving as many as fifty different altar calls. The results were multiplied because the workers had multiplied.

Scholars believe there were more than thirty thousand people in the Jerusalem church and more than one hundred thousand people in the church at Ephesus. The book of Acts never apologizes for or discounts the number of people who came to Christ. Instead, it lists them.

God's Math for Multiplication

God showed me His strategy for multiplication. Each step deals with a different area of math, which will ultimately bring you to the multiplication of your harvest.

1. Addition

You have to start with addition. You cannot multiply before you add. In the body of Christ, addition is where you work, sweat, and give of yourself. You can compare it to going to work every day. You should give 100 percent and do your very best, whether you work in a church or in a secular job. Every two weeks you receive a paycheck. Your check is simple addition. You are never surprised at the amount of money you receive. You know exactly what it will be every time.

2. Subtraction

You may not have realized this, but you have to subtract before you can multiply. What is the first thing you do after you get your paycheck? You immediately start subtracting. You pay your tithes, give offerings, and then pay your bills. You pay the mortgage or rent, gas, electricity, water, sewage, cable, etc.

After your youth ministry is established, one of the first things you will have to learn to do is subtract. How do you do that? The answer lies in Hebrews 12:1: "Let us lay aside every weight, and the sin which doth so easily beset us, and let us run with patience the race that is set before us."

This Scripture speaks of two different things: weights and sin. We all know what sin is. We know when we have done wrong because our conscience pricks us. As you grow in Christ, God will reveal to you the areas in your life that are sinful. What is sin to you today, however, may not have been sinful two years ago.

When I was first saved, I smoked every day and did not think it was wrong. I did not see it as a sin. After a year, God began to deal with me to quit. I knew I needed to be obedient to God. This vice now became a sin to me. When He deals with you about an area of your life, subtract it immediately. If you do not, you will never reach the finish line of the race to which you are called.

There are also weights in our lives and ministry that hold us back. God has dealt with me to remove different weights from my life. I love sports and used to be an ESPN junkie. If I was not playing sports, I watched them on TV.

They were a weight to me. I saw that if I wanted to excel as a youth leader, I could not watch sports for seven hours a day. I needed to spend my free time in the Word and with my family. My love for sports was not a sin but rather a weight that held me down.

You can have weights in your youth ministry as well. A weight might be a dysfunctional department that is not working. It might be something you started but does not work well. For every great success story I have had in ministry, I probably have ten in my closet I would like to forget. They are weights I had to get rid of because they were not working.

Unfortunately, some of your weights can be your workers. You might have leaders who are dragging your program down because they are unfaithful, unproductive, or a gossip. They are hurting your ministry. There will be times when you will have to confront them. If they will not change, then as a leader, you have to make a change.

Students can also become weights. We probably subtract five students a week from Oneighty®. On bad weeks, we subtract ten. This happens for many different reasons. Some are subtracted for misbehavior or for breaking the rules. They can be suspended anywhere from two weeks to one month. In some cases when a serious incident occurs, it might be a year before someone is allowed back.

Subtraction is an ongoing process. You will continually encounter leaders who will drag your ministry down, and students who become distractions to others. As you grow in the Lord, He will show you areas that have become weights. If you are not willing to apply the principle of subtraction in your personal life and ministry, you will never grow into multiplication.

3. Division

What is division? We will continue to use the example of your paycheck. After you have paid your tithe and all of your bills, you then divide up whatever money you have left over. This money goes toward groceries, clothes, recreation, etc. If you are smart, you will wisely invest some of the money and watch it grow exponentially.

The same is true in ministry. You want to properly invest your time in the right people. My time is spent with my staff and the department leaders in Oneighty®. I make sure they have the necessary tools and direction to be successful in what they are doing. I take time to build them up in the Lord.

4. Multiplication

You must first add, subtract, and divide before you can multiply. Once the first three steps have been completed, you divide, delegate, and release your workers into ministry. Only after they step out and work alongside you will you see multiplication in your ministry.

Grow and Maintain Attendance

There are practical steps you can take to experience growth in ministry. After you experience growth, you also want to maintain the numbers. If you put a lot of hard work into a major evangelistic event, you want to see the fruit of your effort stick around.

1. Conduct big events only four to five times a year.

Youth leaders usually make two mistakes when planning events. The first mistake is to plan too many big events. You will constantly have to come up with new hype to continually attract students to each new event. You will actually become your own competition because you are constantly outdoing yourself to keep teenagers interested and the events become ordinary.

It takes a lot of time, money, and planning to put together a good event. You have to let the land rest for a few months in between each big event. Not only are you giving your workers rest, but also each event becomes something special in the minds of your students.

The second mistake is scheduling an event on an off night— not held on the primary meeting night. Typically, youth leaders will hold events on Friday or Saturday night because they think teenagers have extra time on the weekend. Unsaved kids are usually not interested in going to church on a Friday night. They will go to the local football game, especially when it is being played down the street, or on a date. In addition, holding an event on an off night will not help build attendance for the normal meeting night.

We never hold big events on Friday or Saturday nights. Everything we do is held on Wednesday. We do not even hold weekend crusades or activities. We want to build our Wednesday night program so kids get used to coming on that particular night. When you keep the meeting night consistent, they will associate that day of the week with your youth ministry.

2. Use special guests who will appeal to teenagers.

This may shock you, but if you really want a guest who will draw young people, don't invite me. I would love to come, but typically, youth evangelists do not draw kids. Skateboarders and freestyle bikers are popular among our teens. My friend Dennis Rogers, who does feats of strength, was a hit among unsaved and unchurched kids. He has been on the "Late Show with David Letterman" and "LIVE! With Regis & Kathie Lee," and he helped train Evander Holyfield during his boxing career.

Inviting a friend to hear a two-time world skateboarding champion sounds a lot better than coming to hear an evangelist speak. Unsaved kids are not interested in hearing someone talk to them about being saved and avoiding hell. A skateboarding champion who loves the Lord can speak to them about both natural and spiritual matters.

Your guest speakers do not always have to preach. Some of these guys are great at skateboarding, biking, or lifting weights, but are not seasoned preachers. In that case, I usually interview them for fifteen minutes.

We invited Eddie Alvarez, a skateboarder from California, to speak. Eddie is a former world champion and was one of the pioneers of modern skateboarding. In Tony Hawk's recent book, he described Eddie as his idol growing up. The skating community in Tulsa knew who Eddie was and turned out in great numbers.

Before he came up to speak, we showed a taped demonstration of Eddie and me skateboarding on a half-pipe. It was hilarious because I am bad on a skateboard and he is good. After we showed the clip, I interviewed him for ten minutes. He gave his testimony and shared what he felt God was saying to young people today. Afterward, I preached for fifteen minutes. We had over 500 young people give their lives to the Lord that night.

The nights we draw the most teenagers are the nights we hold theme nights. One of our themes was called "Down Under." We told the students we would serve free Joey Strips. They got a kick out of inviting their friends to come and eat kangaroo. (It was actually chicken.) We did a skit that parodied the Australian crocodile wrangler, and I asked an Australian friend, Pat Mesiti, to preach. We had a great turnout. Usually when we have a special theme night, I do not invite a guest speaker but rather speak myself.

3. Carefully follow and analyze your numbers.

Every week we track our attendance and number of visitors. I would suggest putting your numbers in a graph. It is easier to analyze your good and bad months. When you notice a change in your attendance, look to see what you were doing when your numbers jumped as well as when they dropped. Then, do more of whatever caused your attendance to go up, and cut out whatever caused the attendance to drop.

One time Pastor George held a meeting with all the department heads. He told us church attendance had dropped over the past six months. He wanted to find out what was causing people to leave and not come back. After much prayer and discussion, we concluded that the first service was going long. This caused a huge traffic jam between the people leaving the first service and the people trying to get in for the second.

If you have inconveniences in your church or youth group, your core people will put up with it. They are behind you regardless of the hassle. The fringe people will stop coming in a heartbeat. Some people just refuse to be inconvenienced. We made some adjustments in our parking lot regarding the flow of traffic. The change in our parking procedures eliminated much of the traffic hassles. At the same time, Pastor George also made adjustments to make sure the first service was dismissed on time.

Within three weeks, the attendance was back to where it had been, and the church began to grow again. It was a simple alteration. The only reason we noticed a problem was because we were watching our attendance numbers.

Seasons of Growth

You will also find you have seasons of growth and non-growth. For Oneighty®, we typically see a burst of growth in the springtime. When summer hits, our attendance numbers fall through the basement. The first time this happened I thought God had written **Ichabod** across the youth facility. I finally realized over the course of a couple summer campaigns, attendance naturally drops during that time. Families go on vacations or spend weekends at the lake. Church is not a priority for some people during the summer. Moreover, school is out and our campus program is off for the summer.

Numbers also drop between Thanksgiving and the beginning of January. People are busy with the holidays.

With this in mind, we do not plan big events during our down times. In the summer we hold mission trips, outreaches, and summer camp. From Thanksgiving on, we do not have any big events.

4. Provoke your young people with competition.

We hold attendance competitions for big events. The first time we held this type of competition was when we moved into our new auditorium in 1996. Our attendance was around 600, and the new facility seats 1,200.

We wanted to pack the building out for the opening night. We began to brainstorm and came up with the idea of a burger competition. We billed it as a contest between schools to see which students could collectively eat the most. We told the teenagers we would have **thousands** of hamburgers. They could invite all their friends—even the school's football team!

The kids were pumped up, and word of the event took off. We even heard stories of unsaved kids telling their friends about a "hamburger contest at some place called Oneighty®"!

We had 1,553 teenagers show up! The only advertising for the event was by word of mouth among the young people. Of course, all these kids came to eat hamburgers. Most did not know about the service we were having. We held a fun, fast-moving, one-hour meeting. That night 238 teens made first-time decisions for Christ!

The next week our attendance dropped to 800. I was tempted to get discouraged for just a minute. Then I realized the additional 200 students were the ones who gave their lives to the Lord.

Another highly successful competition was the "Battle of the Bulge." We wanted to see which school in Tulsa could bring in the most accumulative weight. We set up scales for each school and each student weighed in at his or her school scale.

We told them it was okay to creatively add weight to themselves without us knowing about it. Some teenagers put rolls of quarters in their pockets and sewed small dumb-bells in their pants. I think a couple of young people brought small transmissions in their backpacks because they tipped themselves at over 300 lbs. They thought of all kinds of ways to weigh themselves down.

At that time we were running around 1,400 kids. The attendance at this event was over 2,500 teenagers. More than 500 young people gave their lives to the Lord that night. At first, I was concerned the theme of the competition would not work. I wondered if kids would want to participate, but they did! It was a huge success!

Competitions are a great way to expose new teenagers to your ministry. Each time we hold one, the numbers increase. We level off afterward, but never to where we were before the event. As you do follow-up with the students who become born again, you will not only add to the kingdom of God, but you will also see your attendance increase.

5. Give teenagers extra incentives to come to church.

We do not do this every week, but on special occasions we give out door prizes. Sometimes we hold a hundred dollar basketball shot. Only students who sat in a chair with a star on the bottom side are given a chance to shoot. The contestants have to complete three stages before they are eligible for the hundred-dollar shot. They have to make a lay-up shot, a foul-line shot, and a three-point shot before trying the half-court shot.

Each basketball shot is awarded a different amount of money. The lay-up shot will garner ten dollars. Most of the teenagers make this shot. They have the choice to keep the money and sit down, or they can try a foul-line shot. If they miss the second shot, they have to return the money. If they make it, we give them another ten dollars. Everyone thinks they can make a foul shot, but only about half of them do.

The successful shooters progress to the three-point line. Again, they are given the choice to keep the money or try this difficult shot. We wave another twenty dollars in front of their eyes. As soon as they see the money, they go for the shot. That is a tough shot, even for a good player. They usually do not make it. Every now and then, we will get a hot shot who does.

I promise you, if a teenager makes the three-point shot, he or she is not able to resist the half-court shot. Before they shoot, they have to give back all the money they won. I then hold up a crisp one hundred dollar bill and tease them with all the things they can buy. Every student who makes it to this point goes for the shot. We have done this several times, but so far we have never given any money away.

On other occasions we rented a Money Machine or a Cash Cube. They come in different shapes but are typically enclosed containers similar to a telephone booth. Some of the portable ones are inflatable and can look like a cash vault, a jukebox, or a slot machine. Instead of money, we put a stack of papers with various prizes written on each sheet and a blower on the inside of the container. A person steps inside and tries to grab as many prizes as he or she can in a short amount of time.

The teenagers who brought the most visitors that night get to go inside the prize machine for ten seconds. Prizes include fast food gift certificates, video games, CD players, clothing store gift certificates, a bunch of one dollar papers that can be added up together for one major gift certificate from our local mall, and a one hundred-dollar piece of paper, as well.

We tell them there are two strategies. Either grab as much paper as you can get your hands on, or keep your eyes open for the hundred-dollar paper and go for that. Everyone tried to find the one hundred-dollar paper. We would get to the end of the countdown and they would finally start grabbing other papers and come out with two or three. Finally, the last kid caught on and walked out with about one hundred dollars in prizes!

The Prize Machine was a blast! The students cheered and went nuts. It also breaks the stereotype of church. Students see going to church can be a blast, as well as spiritual.

6. Host free food nights.

We usually combine a free food night with a big event. We might serve chicken strips, hamburgers, or pizza. It is a great way to draw the unchurched and unsaved young people. They love to eat—especially when it is free.

7. Develop a strong follow-up program.

Tommy Barnett, a First Assembly of God pastor in Phoenix, Arizona, made this statement: "People who are contacted within 24 hours after visiting your church have an 85 percent retention rate." We have developed this same program and found our retention rate is 80 percent. That does not mean 80 percent of the students come all the time, but they come back at least once if we do this.

The program works this way. After we get visitors' names, we contact them three different ways. One may be a personal visit. This visit does not mean we knock on their door. It could be leaving a note and a bag of cookies on the door. We used to put up miniature real estate signs at visitors' homes. The sign had our logo on it and read, "Thank you for coming to Oneighty®. Hope you come back." It was signed by a bunch of our students. After the Wednesday night meeting, a group of teenagers would pound these signs in the yards of all our visitors. Sometimes the sign would be there before the visitor got home.

We do not do this anymore because we have too many first-time visitors, but it was something that made an impression on the visitors as well as their parents. We received many calls from both parents and students thanking us for the sign.

Obviously, another way to contact first-time visitors is through a personal telephone call. We have students call our visitors the next day and thank them for coming. The caller tries to get to know the visitor a little better as well as get their thoughts on Oneighty®. We follow-up with a second telephone call the following week.

Our third point of contact is made through a postcard or letter from me. In it I give them information about Church On The Move and Oneighty®. I let them know how they can plug in.

We are fighting the perception that when someone comes to Oneighty®, they are just a number. We go overboard to give them the assurance that we know who they are. It is imperative, therefore, that you go out of your way to show first-time visitors they are important.

8. Institute a discipleship program.

Pastor George developed an eight-week Oneighty® Discipleship video program. It was designed not only to deepen a teenager's commitment to Christ, but also to deepen their commitment to their local church.

There are different ways you can put your program together. It does not have to be a video program. You can personally teach the classes if you prefer, or you can use audiotapes or CDs. We use videotapes right now.

Each week we give our teenagers a thirty-minute video to take home and watch. The subjects cover foundational truths, such as "How to Resist Temptation," "How to Get Along With Your Parents," "How to Be Filled With the Holy Spirit," and "How to Deal With Authority." While they are enrolled in the discipleship program, we encourage them to commit to:

1 – bring one unchurched friend to Oneighty®

8 – complete the eight-week discipleship program

0 – take the Zero pledge

Upon completion of the program, we bring the graduates before the adult congregation. Pastor George leads them in the following pledge: "From this moment on I will say no to alcohol and drugs. I will have zero nicotine in my life. Zero drugs. Zero alcohol. Zero sexual sin. I will live and remain pure for God from this day forward." This is the heart of Oneighty®.

It is not enough just to draw a crowd. Jesus said to make disciples. We found that moving students through this eight-week program solidifies their relationship with Christ and prepares them to serve in ministry at Oneighty®. Of course, Oneighty® means repentance—to see young people do a one hundred and eighty-degree turn from darkness to light.

Repent is a combination of two words. **"Pent"** is from the word **penthouse,** which means the highest level. If you have a penthouse apartment, you are not in the basement, or even halfway up—you are at the very top! "Re" in repent simply means return. So repent means to return to God's highest level of living, blessing, and abundance. It is a positive word, not a negative one!

Most student discipleship programs I have seen are too difficult for the average Christian young person. Develop an introductory program any teenager can plug into. Once students graduate from our program, we encourage them to serve in a ministry team where the discipleship process continues under their team leader.

9.   Start a bring-a-visitor program.

As an incentive to invite people to Oneighty®, we developed the Oneighty® Mobile Visitor Program. After a student brings eight new visitors to Oneighty®, we roll out the red carpet for them. We pick them and two of their friends up after school in a hot-rod car. First we take them to the Sonic Drive-in for something to eat. Then we take them to their favorite store at the mall.

An inner city youth pastor sent me a picture of the vehicle he uses for his Oneighty® Mobile. He fixed up an old hearse and painted "Life after death. Stop the violence" on the back doors of the vehicle. He works with tough gang kids, and they love being picked up in a hearse. It appeals to the teenagers he works with. You can use any type of car for the Oneighty® Mobile. Whether it is a fancy sports car or an old Chevy you fixed up, your students will love being chauffeured around.

If ever there were a time when we should be concerned about numbers, it is now. While no one knows the exact time in which the Lord will return, everyone agrees it is soon. If you put into practice the steps outlined in this chapter, your youth ministry will grow. It is my desire that multitudes of young people will escape the grip of hell and spend their eternity with our Lord and Savior.

TOUGH QUESTIONS

Q: Can you draw too many unchurched students, resulting in major behavioral problems?

A: If you begin to draw so many unchurched students that they outnumber the core of your Christian kids in an extreme way, then yes, problems can develop. As you grow your numbers, you want to continue to build your core group so they dominate the new kids coming in rather than the opposite.

That happens through ongoing discipleship and making sure the kids coming in are coming to Christ. They should move into a relationship with Christ, into ministry teams, and so on. We have seen different times, especially in the beginning of Oneighty", when we had so many new kids that we had major problems. Kids were found with drugs. Boys were hitting on girls, and gang fights were breaking out. We had to get a handle on it. We had to bring discipline, enforce our rules, and let them know we are in control and they are not. Then we had to strengthen on our discipleship and get kids involved in mentoring through teen ministry.

Yes, you can outgrow your core too quickly and things can get out of control. You want to grow your core as you grow your numbers.

Q: How do you maintain a safe, secure environment for your regular church kids?

A: This is important because you can have a lot of unchurched kids who exhibit behavioral problems and overwhelm your youth group. Parents from your own church will begin to fear dropping off their kids at your youth ministry because they're afraid their kids are going to hear foul language, see things that they shouldn't see, or be around kids they don't want their Christian kids to be around.

You must keep your ministry secure, and you have to deal with behavioral issues that come up. The only way you are going to do that is with a strong monitoring of your facilities and behavior. This starts with your worker team. Make sure you have monitors in every area of your game room and good ushers in your youth meetings to establish control.

As we began to grow into the hundreds of kids at our youth group, we hired off-duty police officers to be there in their police uniforms. It started with a couple, and as we grew larger it become four and then six. It sent a message to the kids that said we are in control here, and we are not going to put up with any bad behavior. It spoke volumes to both our kids and parents that this is going to be a safe and secure place, and as you grow, you may want to consider doing this as well.

Q: Isn't it easy for kids to get lost and unattached in a big youth group?

A: It certainly is if you do not continue to grow small, as you grow big. As your numbers grow, you need to continue developing opportunities for kids to get into a relationship with other kids through smaller groups. For us, those small groups can be identified in a number of different ways.

It may be a ministry team at Oneighty®, such as the greeter team, where kids are serving together as greeters at the doors, and they meet other greeters and build relationships through that team. It may be working in the café team, where they're serving food in the café after the service with a team of other student café workers, and they're building a camaraderie and meeting friends in that ministry. It may be in our campus ministry where they are part of a campus team, where they are meeting once a week in their campus Bible studies and building relationships and teams.

You want to continue to think of different ways you can build student teams and student groups under an adult leader who is responsible, faithful, able to mentor, and able to grow these kids and keep them accountable. You grow large by growing small.

rule ten:

CHaLLenge Your Teens TO WIN THEIr SCHOOLS TO CHrIST

Youth pastors often challenge their young people to be great soul winners in their schools. Who else can better win fellow classmates to the Lord than Christian teenagers? Youth ministries with this attitude closely follow the tenth rule that needs to be broken.

Rule Ten: *Challenge your teens to win their schools to Christ.*

You probably think you should keep this rule. I propose that instead of challenging your teenagers to do this, encourage them to follow the truth that replaces this rule.

Truth Ten: *Send a message that inspires students to win one person to Christ.*

After they have prayed with one person to receive the Lord, inspire them to win someone else.

When you tell your students it is their responsibility to win their school to Christ, you alienate most of them. Two or three of your core teenagers will agree with you and say it is a great idea. However, they probably do not believe they can actually do it. They just like the idea and think it would be cool if it happened.

The remainder of your students will think you are crazy. Some of them are not even living for the Lord yet, and knowing how to lead a person to the Lord is a mystery to them. The very thought of winning an entire school overwhelms them.

We disqualify many candidates for evangelism by making teens feel they have to convert their entire school to Christianity. First they need to be taught how to look for opportunities to share their faith. Then they need to know what to say to lead someone to Christ. After they are taught these things, when you suggest they win one person to Christ, they will have an idea of how to do that. They will have just enough faith to think, *Well, maybe I can.*

Look at your own life. How many people have you won to the Lord since you have been saved? If you were a teenager when you became born again, how many of your fellow students did you persuade to become a Christian?

When I was young, I did not convert my entire school. I tried as hard as I could. I passed out tracts and witnessed to everyone. But I was not successful in convincing everyone at my school to come to Christ.

If you hold a secular job in addition to your youth ministry, have you won your entire workplace to Christ? What about your neighborhood? Have you won your community to the Lord? What about your family? Are they all born again? Most of us are still standing in faith for our families to come to Christ.

It is hypocritical for you to expect your students to change their schools if you have not made an equal impact with everyone you meet. Do not put unrealistic expectations on your teenagers. Rather help them become a better witness for the Lord in their personal lives first. Then show them how to share what God has done for them with others.

Effective Soul Winning

Leading someone to Christ is not hard. Your teenagers will only need the right direction to get started. I have compiled some points that will assist you in teaching your students how to witness to others and reach your community for the Lord.

1. Do not create unrealistic expectations for your teens to live up to. The apostle Paul understood this. In 1 Corinthians 13:11 he said, "When I was a child, I spake as a child, I understood as a child, I thought as a child: but when I became a man, I put away childish things." You have to understand that in the same way young people grow into responsibility, they will also grow into soul winning.

2. When Jesus called Simon Peter and his brother Andrew to be His disciples, He said, "Follow Me, and I will make you fishers of men" (Matt. 4:19). He was saying He would show them how to win souls. Using this Scripture as our foundation, we use our summer mission program as a way to teach and develop soul winners.

I love summer missions for several reasons. We are winning the lost and fulfilling the great commission. When young people come back from a mission trip, they return better than when they left. Their thought patterns and priorities change on these trips. After they get back, they are pumped up and ready to set the world on fire. We take this excitement and channel it so they can make an impact in their families and at their schools.

It is difficult to change a student's life in one night. When you have them for only one hour a week, it takes a long time before you see any dramatic change in their life. During a weekend camp, you can put more into them. You can have the greatest impact on their lives when you are able to work with them during a two-week or month-long mission trip. They are with you constantly, and you have the opportunity to mentor and disciple them. This experience can change their habits and lifestyle patterns. Once they return home, their family and friends will be able to see a noticeable difference in their lives.

One-on-One Training

When we are on a mission trip, we require the teenagers to get up early for devotions. This may be the first time they have disciplined themselves to read their Bible every day. Afterward, we send them out to win souls.

We start our street or village ministry at a public school. We always present a drama because it is a good way to draw a crowd of kids. After the skit we tell the assembly we want to talk to them about God and what He has done in our lives. The teenagers then go into the crowd and share their faith.

We usually have one or two teenagers who sit back because they do not have the boldness to step out and witness. Our leaders look for these students. At first they have the teens watch and listen as they witness. Then the leader with them tells them to say something to the next person they witness to. If they say only two words, that is all right. The leader will tell them how anointed they were for those four seconds and encourage them to say a little bit more the next time.

Each time one of these timid young people share, we tell them what they said was great. We might remind them of a Scripture they could use the next time. We keep doing this until finally after three or four times of sharing their faith, the student has a handle on witnessing. Once they are at a point where they are doing all the talking, we do not have to work with them again. In fact, they will grab their friends and show them how to bring someone to the Lord.

It is a mentoring process. A leader does not usually have to stay with them long before they are ready to be released. Jesus did the same with His disciples. They were with Him constantly and watched everything He did. He gave them opportunities to minister while He was with them before sending them out on their own. (Matt. 10:1.)

If you have never taken your young people on a mission trip, I would suggest going with a teen mission organization for your first time out. You can hook up with many good organizations. They have taken these trips for years and know the secret ingredients that make a great mission trip. Watch what they do and learn from them. Later, you can develop your own program.

3. Target your outreach so you can provide effective discipleship follow-through. When we go on an outreach, our goal is more than conversion. We do not want to pray the sinner's prayer with a lot of people if we cannot also do follow-through. If they cannot become plugged into a church, the opportunity for them to fall away from Christ is too great.

Although many street people hang in the downtown area of Tulsa, I never take our teenagers street witnessing there. We do not have discipleship follow-through for that type of ministry. If an organization with a ministry to the homeless called us for help, we could assist them because they would provide the necessary discipleship follow-through.

Outreach is more than praying a prayer and sending people on their way. Before you launch into a ministry, make sure you can properly follow through. You always want to be able to disciple all your new converts. We do the evangelism in places where we know we can follow-up. For us, that is in our campus ministry and at the juvenile detention center. When we go on a mission trip, we work with host missionaries. They already have a follow-up program set in place.

4. God calls young people arrows. They are meant to fly fast and make an impact. Psalm 127:4 says, "As arrows are in the hand of a mighty man; so are children of the youth." This Scripture is simply saying young people are called to go make an impact. I believe our teenagers can be some of the greatest evangelists of our day.

We have to remember that an arrow is crafted. Today we simply buy arrows. In the days of the Old Testament, they had to work to fine-tune the arrow so it would fly straight.

The same is true with our young people. We have to work with them. When they are released into ministry, they will soar straight and true like a well-crafted arrow.

5. Create a campus ministry focused on invitation first and then conversion. We want our students to be able to lead their friends to Christ. Some of our kids, however, are not there yet, but they can invite someone to Oneighty®. Our free games are a good drawing point to help them. I tell them they do not even have to mention the fact that I will preach. They only have to get their friends here any way they can. Once they come, God will deal with their hearts.

Our bus ministry started because of our challenge to teenagers to invite their friends to Oneighty®. When we started we needed only one bus to pick up teenagers. Today we use up to thirty buses a week.

6. A student's home is a neutral, non-threatening gathering location for unchurched teens. Our buses do not pick up young people at the school campuses. We hold pre-game meetings on Wednesday night from 5:30 to 6:30 at the home of a student. The students are picked up around 6:30 and are brought to Oneighty®. After the service, the buses take them back to the student's home and their parents pick them up there.

The pre-game home is a great place because it is a neutral location. Parents who are sending their unchurched kids know they are going to "Jimmy Smith's" home. It is a little less non-threatening for an unchurched kid. These smaller groups are also a great place to build relationships as your ministry grows in size.

7. Effective campus ministry begins with zealous students coached by committed adults. We have tried to start campus ministries with only committed adults, but it does not work that way. Until you have a couple of zealous students, your campus ministry will not take off.

One campus ministry started with two people. The teens were excited, and we kept encouraging them. We helped them by giving them flyers and brochures. They did all the work, and in one year their ministry grew to eighty kids.

8. Start home Bible studies for each campus ministry team for training, accountability, and strategizing. In addition to the home gathering on Wednesday nights, we hold a Bible study on Monday and Tuesday nights. The kids from each campus

ministry come together to pray and study the Word. They also strategize to come up with new ways to reach their school through campus ministry.

9. Solve the problem of transportation in your community. Many young people would love to come to your youth group but do not have a way of getting there. When we started using transportation to bring the kids to our service, our numbers shot up.

If your church does not have a bus or van you can use, stand in faith for God to provide you with transportation. One youth pastor in Texas told me he negotiated with the owner of a car rental agency. He wanted to rent twelve vans every Wednesday night. The owner did not have any demand for the vans on Wednesday night, so he gave this youth pastor an unbelievable discount! Within a matter of months, this youth pastor was transporting 300 new students to church every week. If you have the vision, God will bring the provision!

There are different ways to solve your transportation problem. Typically, we think we have to buy a van or a bus. Allow the Lord to move on your behalf. You never know how He will turn your situation around.

10. Finally, challenge your students to stop inviting their friends to church! I preached a two-part message with this theme and at first my kids thought I had lost my mind. Stop inviting friends to church? I took my text from Luke 14 where the master puts on a great feast and tells his servant to invite guests. The servant goes out to issue invitations, but came back with only excuses. The master gets angry and gives him a new strategy. He now tells the servant to go to every highway, hedge, and alley and **bring** them to the dinner—**compel** them to come! So I challenged our Oneighty® students to stop inviting and start bringing. Inviting is a part of the process of evangelism, but not everything. I used the word **bring** to make five key points in compelling friends to come to church.

B. Begin to pray for them. Pray for their eyes to be opened to their need for Christ and for the blinders to come off. (2 Cor. 4:4.)

R. Remember to plan. Let God show you a plan to reach each person. A good fisherman knows exactly what kind of hook and bait will work for certain kinds of fish!

I. Invite them to come.

N. Never give up. Even if they don't come the first time, keep asking! A study of national sales executives found that in most cases it takes five calls to the same prospect to get the sale. We must be persistent.

G. Get their commitment. Don't just hope they show up. Go to their house and pick them up. Do not allow them any way to get out. When you set a fish on your hook, you have to keep the line tight and reel it in. Fish don't jump in the boat by themselves.

God has done so much in our lives that it should be natural to share our testimonies with others. Most people need instruction on how to effectively witness to others. By following the points outlined in this chapter, you will help your students overcome their insecurities and step out into evangelism.

TOUGH QUESTIONS

Q: What practical steps can I take to do a summer missions trip for our students?

A: First, take your group with another organization. Early on at Oneighty®, we went on our first mission trip with Teen Mania Missions, Ron Luce's organization. We took a two-week trip to Haiti and learned with our leaders how to do missions. We saw the key ingredients to a successful trip, and someone like Teen Mania, who has done mission trips for nearly twenty years, knows what they are doing and how to put a good trip together. You can learn a lot by going with someone else first. Then go a second or third year and maybe work with one of the missionaries your church supports.

I would try to find a missionary in South America—Guatemala, Peru, or Mexico—because it is closer and less expensive. People there are very hungry to receive the gospel, so you are going to have a good harvest and see good results, which is important. You want to encourage your kids by seeing good results.

Keep your trip between ten and fourteen days. Include about three days of training at your church or a camp before you leave just to make sure everyone is on board and you are strong. Set the guidelines. If you're doing a drama, learn your drama. Work with your missionary to set up an itinerary of the days you will be there so you can perform two or three outreaches a day at villages, prisons, or schools. If kids are in school, arrange for a place to have the assemblies at schools. Make sure you incorporate into each week at least one day off for fun, relaxation, refreshing, and just having a good time with your kids.

At the end of your trip, debrief your kids and talk about what they have learned. Prepare them to reenter the mainstream of America and take what they have learned to reach their friends back home.

Q: My students are "fired up" to reach their friends after a camp or special event, but their zeal quickly tapers off. How do I keep them motivated?

A: The best way to keep our kids motivated in evangelism is to develop teams on each campus you are trying to reach. The ministry team starts with an adult leader willing to commit to the students in that school. This requires going to the school almost every week, having lunch with the kids, or attending a football game on a Friday night. They are responsible for a Bible study each week or two at a home in the area, preferably the home of a student or parent from your church.

Strategizing, planning, studying the Word together, developing relationships, and talking about how can we reach and touch more and more kids in each school is important. Then build student leaders and encourage those student leaders to take ownership to reach their campus.

Doing this helps keep the fires burning. Leaders are responsible for motivating and going after the kids each week. They work the phones, and have their key student leaders help them work the phones. They begin to develop other adult leaders so there's three or four other adult leaders working with them in that school. If you've got someone regularly keeping those kids accountable, pouring fuel on their fire so the fire doesn't go out, it will help your kids keep the passion, fire, and zeal throughout the school year.

Q: Do you try to get your students to start Christian clubs on their campus?

A: Today, most campuses already have a Christian club. Rather than start another one or try to compete, we try to encourage them to support the club already in place. If there is not a club going and they have a heart to start one, we will certainly help them every way we can, and provide resources and tools. Most of the time there is already a club, so get there, support the club, and add to it every way you can.

Our focus with campus ministry is to encourage the kids to reach out and bring friends who need Christ every week. Ultimately, the local church is where lives are changed. Jesus said, "I am building my church, and the gates of hell will not prevail against it." (Matt. 16:18.) We want to build the church, and the only way we can do that is to get kids in church. That is our focus.

effective marketing

LET PEOPLE KNOW YOU EXIST

There is a reason why companies spend millions of dollars to buy one thirty-second commercial on Super Bowl Sunday—marketing is powerful. Jesus told His disciples to shout from the housetops what He told them in secret. (Matt. 10:27.) During Jesus' day, vendors marketed their goods from the rooftops of their homes or places of business. They would shout out to passers-by what they had to sell and how much they wanted for their product. All the business owners advertised their products this way.

Jesus was advising us in Matthew 10:27 to use the marketing tools that are available to us. How do we shout from our rooftops today? There are a variety of methods in which we can advertise. Most youth ministries do not have large advertising budgets, so you need to be wise in how and where you spend your money. I have put together some points that work for us. I believe they will help you in your efforts to come up with ingenious ways to market and advertise your ministry.

1. Do not promote or advertise youth meetings until your teenagers are unashamed to bring their friends.

First things first. Work on your facilities and your program before you begin to advertise. When you have a quality program and facility, your teenagers will want to bring their friends.

2. Teenage consumers will buy your look and sound before they ever consider your message.

Kids are not interested in buying your message. Your look and sound are what attract them. After you have gotten their attention, only then will they look at your message. When I say look and sound, I am talking about your graphic design with printed invitations and the production quality of other media, like radio and television. We are wasting our money if we don't do things right.

3. Be sure all your advertising passes the "cool" test.

I would rather not advertise at all than put out an advertising piece that is cheesy. You are only hurting yourself when you put out inferior advertising. It is better to do one good advertising piece a year than twenty bad ones.

4. Decide which form of advertising is best for you.

My personal recommendation to any youth ministry is to develop an invitation tool. Teenagers are your best method of marketing your ministry to other teenagers. Having a tool to put into their hands makes it easier for them to invite their friends to your youth meetings.

Bulletins

Weekly bulletins are effective and inexpensive ways to advertise. Although several of them will end up on your floor before the service is over, many will make it into the homes of students. When that happens, it may find its way into a parent's hand. They will then learn what is going on in the youth department.

In these bulletins, we do fun things like competitions to see who can pick the winning brackets for the Final Four Basketball Tournament. I hope a teenager will hold on to it a little longer because it is not just a bunch of boring announcements week after week. A student might be at school talking to a friend trying to decide which team will win. The bulletin could open a door to tell his friend about Oneighty® and invite him to church. We do whatever we can to give our young people opportunities to talk about Oneighty® to their friends.

Postcards

We have developed a formula for advertising that we call "HYPE." It means to publicize, promote, or exploit by touting. We use it in all our advertising. The "School's Back" postcard is a good example of how HYPE works.

"H" stands for "headline." Make your headlines bold. In our postcard, "School's Back!" is bold.

"Y" stands for "you guarantee." Make a guarantee when you advertise. What are you going to do to help your consumer? We guaranteed Oneighty® would relieve the pain of going back to school.

school's BACK.

oneighty can RELIEVE the pain.

oneighty® can serve your ever growing needs every **WEDNESDAY and SATURDAY night at 7 p.m.** beginning august 29.

to physically be at oneighty® exit I-244 at garnett, drive 2,395 feet north to e. marshall (interchange business park). every week tulsa does a oneighty®. where have you been?

(Oneighty)®

youth ministry of Church On The Move
P.O. Box 770 Tulsa, OK 74101

9 out of 10 Doctors we've talked to prescribe high dosages of Oneighty® to relieve school pain. here's why:

1) A lot of cool people just like you.
2) Loud music is encouraged.
3) +35 free arcade games.
4) Absolutely no homework.
5) Two indoor basketball courts.
6) Great food for about $1.
7) Inspiration to get you through the week.
8) Laughing out loud won't land you in the principal's office.

For more great facts call: the Oneighty® info line at **234-8180**

SURGEON GENERALS WARNING: Quitting school greatly increases your chances of being a total moron. Go to Oneighty® instead.

"P" stands for "package benefits." On the reverse side of the postcard, we listed the benefits of coming to Oneighty®. To an unchurched audience, the benefits are not "come and get saved" or "learn how to obey your parents." Adults will think this is a benefit, but young people do not. All your advertisements need to be written from a teenager's point of view. This is how we listed the benefits of Oneighty®.

"Nine out of ten doctors prescribe high dosages of Oneighty® to relieve school pain. Here's why....."

1. A lot of people just like you.

2. Loud music is encouraged.

3. +35 free arcade games.

4. Absolutely no homework.

5. Two indoor basketball courts.

6. Great food for about $1.

7. Inspiration to get you through the week.

8. Laughing out loud won't land you in the principal's office.

These eight points let teenagers know they can hang out with other young people at Oneighty®; they will hear great music and have plenty of games to play. These are benefits from a non-religious perspective.

"E" stands for "easy action." You have to provide an easy way for young people to act on your advertising. Regardless of what you do, provide a way they can find out more information to be a part of your youth group. Our action line says, "For more great facts call the Oneighty® info line at 234-8180." The information line is a pre-recorded line and gives the caller information about Oneighty® as well as directions to our facility. You could also use a web address with the same function.

The postcard is sent to anyone who has ever come to Oneighty®. If you do not have a mailing list, create a form and have all your students write their names and addresses on it. There are different computer programs on the market that can help you track your students. I would recommend getting one of these programs and inputting all their names into a database. Then, as new kids come, add their information to the mailing list.

Radio and Television

There are two philosophies in radio and TV advertising I call blanket and blast. Anyone who sells either medium will tell you if you want to reach your community, you have to do *blanket* advertising. They want you to buy several spots every day for as many weeks as possible. We have tried this, but it has not worked for us. We advertised month after month with generic ads about Oneighty®. Our attendance never went up at all. We spent thousands of dollars getting our name out there but did not see any results from it.

We then started **blast** advertising. When we have a major event—a guest speaker or a theme night—we will blast the airwaves for one week. Teenagers do not make plans for more than a couple of days in advance. If you buy two weeks of advertising, you wasted your money on the first week, and it is better to have a high concentration of radio spots a couple of days right before the event. If you advertise this way, radio will work and you will have an increase in your attendance on those nights.

The only way I would buy more than a week of advertising is for a major concert event. If we brought in someone like the Newsboys, it would take time for people to buy tickets. If I thought there would be a rush to get tickets, I might do two or three weeks of advertising.

We do some television advertising but not a lot. Depending on which cable company you advertise, you can have hundreds of stations to choose from. Keep in mind that most teenagers change channels once a commercial comes on. Even though your commercial is on a popular teen station, you are not guaranteed your target audience will see it.

Tulsa has a local TV station that airs the top high school football and basketball games each week. Oneighty® is one of the sponsors for this program. We hit our target audience. Tulsa high school kids and their parents watch these games all the time. It is also inexpensive TV advertising.

We once advertised during the MTV Awards. We found it was cheaper to buy airtime on MTV than it was to buy time on ABC, CBS, or one of our local channels. Cable TV advertising can be very inexpensive because there are so many stations—they are selling airtime at bargain prices.

When choosing television time, look for niches where you know kids will be watching. When we advertised during the MTV Awards, we knew we were strongly hitting our target audience. You just have to be careful and put some thought behind how and when you advertise on TV.

Internet

Teenagers love the Internet and are always surfing on it. Many people now turn to the Internet to get information. It is relatively easy to build a simple web site. Many companies can do it for you. Again, you want something that is slick to attract young people.

Billboards

We advertised for two years on a billboard outside one of the local malls. This type of advertising can be expensive, with advertising costs anywhere from one to three thousand dollars a month. Billboards do not cause young people to come to your youth group, but they give you credibility. When we started going into the schools, teachers were more favorable toward us because they saw our billboard.

A good way to get ideas on how to advertise to the youth culture is by following the secular advertisement geared toward teenagers. Pick up teen and sports magazines and listen to teen radio stations. They spend hundreds of thousands of dollars doing market research to find out what appeals to teenagers. Use their advertisement as a source of inspiration to come up with ideas on how to reach the young people in your community.

TOUGH QUESTIONS

Q: How would you advertise for one of your "big nights"?

A: There are four things we do to promote a big night. We keep a mailing list and add all new visitors to that list. We send out a postcard advertising the big night a couple weeks in advance to our entire mail list.

We supply all our students with a "bringvitation." It is an invitation, but we call it a bringvitation because we want them not to just invite, but to bring someone. The card is about 3" x 3", and it usually has a cool picture of our guest on the front or some kind of theme reflected in the picture. The other half contains information about what's going to happen that night and directions to the location. We have thousands of those printed. The kids take twenty, thirty, or forty at a time, put them in their purse or pocket, and pass them out to their friends.

We promote for one week on radio, starting seven days out. We target a radio station that core students listen to in the city.

I proclaim the vision of what we are going to do on this big night for about two weeks. In the services leading up to that big night, I tell the kids, "Hey, it's going to be a great night. It is going to be big. It is going to be incredible and you don't want to miss it, so bring a friend.

I give them a goal; for instance, seeing a hundred young people respond to the altar call that night. That's not going to happen unless they bring people who need Christ. We really proclaim the vision and get them on board.

Q: I have never seen any Oneighty® promotional material with clip art. Where do you get your cool photos and graphic look?

A: We don't use clip art. If you look at all the major magazines in the market place today geared towards teenagers, they don't use clip art either. It doesn't work. Today's kids are a little bit sharper than that, and you have to produce something sharp if they are going to be reached.

A lot of our advertising is photo driven. Today's kids love promotional pieces that have cool photos. We actually have a photographer in town that we use to take photos of kids and cool things we think we can use multiple times in our promotion. You can also get photos on the Internet. We do this quite a bit. You can purchase photography for as little as twenty-five dollars for use in your youth group.

There is literally nothing you can't buy today in terms of photos—everything from elephants, cool cars, cool kids, and old people who are not cool. There are many different things you can do to produce some really great graphic looks.

Q: Do you ever let outside groups use your game facility to help promote your cause in the community?

A: We do, but only when we are in control of what happens that night. Let me give you an example. This fall during the school year, we did something we have never done before. We set aside our Tuesday and Thursday nights, which are off nights for us, and invited the varsity football teams from all the major public schools in town to come. We allocated one school a night to just hang out and use our game room. We fed them hamburgers, and the church incurred the cost. We didn't charge them anything. We asked them if we could give them a motivational talk that night on success.

After an hour in the game room and eating hamburgers, we took about 50 to 70 players into our auditorium. We showed video snippets that talked about Oneighty®, nothing that preached at them, and then we had a guest speak. We came to know a former NFL player, Dennis Byrd, who has a wonderful testimony. He shared at several of these events about leadership and what it takes to succeed in life. He spoke from his experiences and on leadership principles that were true, but he didn't preach at the kids.

We introduced their head coach and he shared for a few minutes with the team, then we let them go home. It was a time of influence. We were not trying to get them saved or preach at them, but to influence them. We let them know at the end of the night, "Hey, guys, every Wednesday night, we're here, and if you are ever looking to meet a bunch of really cool kids, Oneighty® Wednesday nights are for anyone. You don't have to be a church kid to come."

We have seen coaches come back to our church the next week and receive Christ. Students come back to Oneighty® in the weeks following and receive Christ. This has worked extremely well.

the "ten demandments"

The "Ten Demandments" are laws to keep for successful, step-by-step youth ministry construction. We have talked about ten time-honored rules that need to be broken in order to succeed and grow your local ministry. I want to conclude this book by talking about these "Ten Demandments."

The Lord spoke to Job three different times trying to correct him and put him on the right track.

> Then the Lord answered Job out of the whirlwind and said, who is this that darketh council by words without knowledge? Gird up now thy loin like a man: for I will demand of thee, and answer thou me (Job 38:1-3 KJV.)

Two more times in Job 40:7 and Job 42:4, God speaks straight to His servant, using the word "demand." God placed some strong demands on Job and had some high expectations for him. And because Job eventually responded the right way and followed God's instruction, the Lord was able to not only restore, but double the blessings in his life.

If you are going to succeed in ministry, not only will you be required to break some time-honored, traditional rules, but you will also have to allow God to place demands on you and those assisting you. It is time to step things up—gird up our loins and be men and women of God. We can't settle for mediocrity anymore. We must demand excellence in all we do, God's very best. So here are the "Ten Demandments" for effective, fruitful youth ministry.

These are demands I believe you must make of yourself, your youth ministry, and your church in order to succeed. They are the next steps to take to effect change in your youth group, to see more kids won to Christ and discipled, and to see your youth group explode. Let's begin with demand number one.

Demandment Number 1: I Will Be Loyal.

You must demand loyalty of yourself, your team, your pastor, and your church. Growth in your youth ministry requires unity. If you are not supportive of the church's vision as well as your pastor's vision, you limit your success.

The Bible says in 1 Corinthians 1:10 NKJV, "Now I plead with you, brethren, by the name of our Lord Jesus Christ, that you all speak the same thing, and that there be no divisions among you, but that you be perfectly joined together in the same mind and in the same judgment." As your pastor leads your church, it is important that you are joined together. We have an incredible power when we are unified.

> And when the day of Pentecost was fully come, they were all with one accord in one place. And suddenly there came a sound from heaven as of a rushing mighty wind, and it filled all the house where they were sitting (Acts 2:1-2 KJV).

The disciples were in one place and one accord and suddenly there was a mighty rushing wind that filled the house. The Holy Spirit moved and the day of Pentecost came when the disciples were in one accord, thinking the same thing, with the same mind and judgment. They were going the same direction, and God began to move.

As you come into unity and support with your church and pastor, you are going to see great things happen.

The Bible says there should be no division among us. (1 Cor. 1:10 NKJV.) When you study the word **division,** you will find it is a combination of two words: "di" and "vision." "Di" means divide, or two.

If you have division, you have two visions, or a divided vision that will go different directions. You do not want to bring division into your church. You want to have one vision—uni-vision. You should go the same direction as your pastor, because ultimately your pastor answers to the head of the church, the Lord Jesus Christ, and leads that church as Jesus has spoken to him. Unity will put you on the same page.

Three areas of unity I believe are important to have with your church and your pastor are philosophical, doctrinal, and staff unity. Philosophical unity affirms you are leading the same way your pastor leads. My pastor has a staff meeting with all church staff and key department leaders every Tuesday morning. I lead just like he leads; therefore, every Wednesday morning I do the same thing with our Oneighty® staff.

I have made a decision to lead the same way my pastor leads. I have followed and studied his leadership style. I want to confront, mentor, and lead by his example. I have taken his philosophical styles and applied them in the way I lead as well. Philosophically, it is important that you are in unity with your pastor.

The second area is doctrinal unity. I listen to what my pastor preaches. I know what he believes and make sure the doctrine I bring into our young people is in agreement with what my church and pastor believe. I receive from him; then I take the things I hear in his messages and his personal mentoring, and pass those doctrines and teachings on to our young people. We have unity in our doctrine.

Third, it is important that we have staff unity. I want to be certain I do not cause divisions among our staff. There are people who say, "I'm true to my pastor," but then they cause strife with other staff members. They don't treat people in the church or other staff members as they should.

Jesus said, "And the King shall answer and say unto them, Verily I say unto you, Inasmuch as ye have done it unto one of the least of these my brethren, ye have done it unto me" (Matt. 25:40).

When you mistreat staff in your church, not only are you doing it to Jesus, but you are literally mistreating your pastor, because they are an extension of him. Make sure you flow with the other teams in the church. The Christian education department, ushers, altar counselors, and those that are involved in missions and seniors' ministry all need to see the big picture together. You are serving each other's departments. You are working together and supporting one another so you don't allow yourself to bring division among the team.

Stay in unity; speak the same thing. Be of the same mind and support your pastor. As you give support, you will reap support in your ministry. Demand loyalty of yourself and your team members. Make sure the leaders under you, volunteer workers, and your staff are supportive. Unity across the board assures strength in your ministry.

Demandment Number 2: I Will Build My Core.

Demand commitment from your core. The second great demand you have to do to grow your ministry, to go forth, to build and construct a strong successful youth ministry, is a demand of commitment from the core of your kids and your leaders. Don't try to reach the masses until you have first reached your church kids.

God told Joshua:

> No man shall be able to stand before you all the days of your life. As I was with Moses, so I will be with you. I will not leave you nor forsake you, be strong and of good courage **for to this people** you shall divide as an inheritance the land which I swore to their fathers to give them."

Joshua 1:5,6

God told Joshua to be strong and of good courage. He promised to be with him just like He was with Moses. God instructed him to be strong for his people.

He told him, "Before you think about going after the walled cities, invading the land of Canaan and overcoming that land to take that inheritance, remember you are going to do it with your people. Explain the vision to them and get them on board, Joshua. Be strong for them so they can go with you."

If you are going to reach your community, schools, and city, you have to have your kids on board. It will take a team. You are going to have to build a solid leadership and student core.

If you want to build that team, you can do something we did at the very beginning of Oneighty®. For four successive weeks, we conducted a survey in our church. We put a survey form in the Sunday bulletin and said to the parents each week, "If you have a teenager who is going to our church, or maybe they're not going right now but you come as a parent, we want to know who they are. Write down their name, address, and phone number down and put it in the offering this week or drop it at the information desk."

We did this over the course of several weeks because some people don't come to church every week. As the survey information came in, we found there were hundreds of kids in our church who did not attend youth group although their parents attended our church. We realized we had a job to do to reach our church kids. Before we start to reach the lost and evangelize to the masses, let's reach the core.

Our survey results helped us develop a strategic plan of how we could get these kids to our youth services. We held a mail campaign, a phone campaign, and planned a big night to invite all these kids to the grand opening of Oneighty®. We said, "Listen, you're the core. You are students who are already involved in our church, or your parents are already involved, and we want to bring you in and let you know you are an important part. We want to give you an assignment and help you find your place. You are important to us." We had a big meeting to bring all the core kids together.

Then we brought our core leaders together through announcements in our church. We said, "If you want to serve in this incredible new youth ministry, come for a special leadership meeting." The core leaders who were already there, the ones who wanted to be added, and the new ones we could get in met for a training night.

We pronounced a vision which included where we were going with new direction for our ministry. We proclaimed, "It's going to be better than ever!" We had a launch date for a brand new ministry on this date. We gave them job assignments, opportunities to serve, and ownership of the ministry. We said, "We're going to do this together."

We told the old guard of students and leaders, "Listen, things are going to change around here. We're getting ready to do something totally different."

I must be honest. As Pastor George prepared to introduce Oneighty®, not all the young people or leaders were excited about it. They thought *Well, what's wrong with our old youth group? We liked it the way it used to be.* You will always have that old guard, but you have to tell them, "Hey, we're going to the next step."

Just like when Joshua prepared to lead the people into the Promised Land, there were people who liked where they were. You have to tell them, "This is going to be worth the change and the sacrifice to do this next step to reach more kids than we've ever reached before." Tell them you need them to come on board and do their job. Rally your core before you begin to reach the masses. You have to demand commitment from your core.

Demandment Number 3: I Will Alter Our Image.

The third thing you have to demand if you are going to birth a brand new ministry is a new image. If you want to start things new, then give your ministry a new name and a new look.

If you are a mother or father, when you give birth to a new baby you do not just call it "human," you give it a fresh, new name. A new ministry deserves a good name, because the name is important.

Jesus put a lot of emphasis on a good name. In Matthew 16, Jesus was about to birth a new thing called "The Church." He said, "Listen, Simon, I am building my church, and the gates of hell will not prevail against it." (Matt. 16:18.) Up to that point, there had never been a church. Then He said, "You are Peter, and upon this rock I will build my church. From now on, you are no longer Simon; you're Peter, which means "Little Rock." Jesus gave him a brand new name. He said, "I want you to call yourself Peter from this time on." Names are important.

The Bible says in Proverbs 22:1, "A good name is to be chosen, even more than great riches." Keep the new name for your ministry simple. The names we choose are easy to remember. Oneighty® comes off the lips of young people easily. We have a national youth conference each year in March called **Elevate.** It is a simple name.

Our Junior High ministry is called Genesis, again a very simple name. Genesis means the beginning of Oneighty®. As the Junior High students come in, they are the Genesis of Oneighty®. So keep it simple, keep it fresh, yet make your name relevant and meaningful.

Your look is important for a new ministry as well. Work on developing a cool logo for your name and give your facility a new appearance.

Take a look at yourself and determine if you need to make some changes. Maybe you decide, *Hey, I'm gonna look at the way I dress, look at my hairstyle, and keep myself in shape physically. As we're doing a makeover within our ministry maybe I personally need a makeover.*

I am not saying you need to get your ears pierced, a tongue ring, or color your hair purple. I don't think you need to look, act, and dress like a teenager to reach teenagers. But it doesn't hurt for us to evaluate ourselves from time to time.

As you begin to launch a new ministry, look at the appearance and image of your ministry, your name, your facility, and even yourself and your worker team. We had nice golf shirts made for our worker team with the Oneighty® logo on the chest. The appearance of our workers changed. The total new appearance gave everyone a new start and a fresh sense of excitement.

In 2 Chronicles 2:5 Solomon said, "In the temple which I build will be great, for our God is greater than all gods." I love that attitude. He said, "Listen, our God is great, so we are going to build a great temple."

I believe we need to have that attitude with our facility and the things we do. We are serving a great God. Jesus is awesome. Let's represent Him with excellence in all that we do.

Solomon built the temple, and it was so great that the Queen of Sheba came in, looked around, and it literally says that her breath was taken away. She was so blown away by it that she gave Solomon a great offering because she wanted to support what he had built.

> And when the queen of Sheba had seen all Solomon's wisdom, and the house that he had built, And the meat of his table, and the sitting of his servants, and the attendance of his ministers, and their apparel, and his cupbearers, and his ascent by which he went up unto the house of the LORD; there was no more spirit in her. And she said to the king, It was a true report that I heard in mine own land of thy acts and of thy wisdom. Howbeit I believed not the words, until I came, and mine eyes had seen it: and, behold, the half was not told me: thy wisdom and prosperity exceedeth the fame which I heard. Happy are thy men, happy are these thy servants, which stand continually before thee, and that hear thy wisdom. Blessed be the LORD thy God, which delighted in thee, to set thee on the throne of Israel: because the LORD loved Israel for ever, therefore made he thee king, to do judgment and justice. And she gave the king an hundred and twenty talents of gold, and of spices very great store, and precious stones: there came no more such abundance of spices as these which the queen of Sheba gave to king Solomon (1 Kings 10:4-10).

This ungodly queen wanted to support what Solomon had done. As you build a great ministry in excellence, because our God is excellent, you will attract many people who want to support it.

Demandment Number 4: I Will Launch.

The fourth demand you're going to have to make of your ministry as you begin to go to the next level and reach more kids is to demand a launch night that will blow everyone away. It will kick off everything in a big way.

You want a grand opening that inspires people and motivates your church, as well as your students and leaders. When everyone shows up on that first big night and sees the facility for the first time, everyone walks away saying, "Wow! I can't wait to tell my friends about this." It spills over with good emotions and favor in your community. People will talk about it and it will bring a new beginning in your ministry.

Nehemiah rallied the people and said, "Hey, we're gonna rebuild the walls." It was hard work and took much effort, but finally, the wall was finished.

At the dedication of the wall of Jerusalem they sought the Levites out, of all their places, to bring them to Jerusalem, to keep the dedication with gladness, both with thanksgivings, and with singing, with cymbals, Psalteries, and with harps" (Neh. 12:27).

They told as many people as possible. They invited everyone in and had a huge celebration. This is the right thing to do. Have a big launch for a new ministry and a new facility. Let your city know about it. Advertise and promote it. Let your whole church know about it. Tell everyone to "Come on out."

Make sure you allow the teenagers to have the good seats. Tell the adults "If you have to stand at the back or in the overflow area, that's fine, but we want you all to see what happens this first night."

Invite the city leaders. Include the mayor, governor, congressmen, and senators, as well as educators. These leaders might help give you favor in the days to come and open other doors for you. Recognize them when they come in that night. Make sure you have free food for everyone.

Take that night, as you preach, to proclaim the vision of your ministry: what you're going to do and what it's there for. Be bold to talk about the Lord and what Christ wants to do in the lives of young people.

We rented searchlights when we launched Oneighty®. It builds a sense of excitement as people are coming in. They see the searchlights in the evening sky and think, *Man, this is huge. This is big. This is extraordinary.*

As you come together to launch your new ministry and your new facility, have your leaders drape a ribbon across the stage, and pray as you dedicate that facility to Christ. You are committing to God to reach young people and to disciple students. Have your pastor and key leaders cut that ribbon for an official launching.

Take time that night to honor those who have sacrificed with extra effort to build the facility and prepare for this moment. Thank those publicly who made significant contributions. You can give plaques or special gifts to say thank you to those who helped you make the night possible.

So, as you launch, make it a big night. Make it a night where dreams are fulfilled and vision is accomplished. Then build on that success to go even further in the days ahead.

Demandment Number 5: I Will Invest.

The fifth demand you have to place on your ministry is a financial demand—a commitment to put the resources you need into your youth ministry to grow.

When I say to demand financial commitment from your church I don't mean to walk into your pastor's office and say, "Pastor, I demand money for this ministry. You'd better give me all the money I need."

You must trust God and believe Him. Go to God with your desires in prayer. The Scripture promises to meet all our needs according to His riches in glory. (Phil. 4:19.) That includes our needs in youth ministry!

Place a demand on that promise, believe God, and say, **Lord, You promised to meet our needs; and therefore, I believe that these needs are being met, in Jesus' name.** What if your pastor hasn't been very financially supportive in the past? It is important to be honest with your pastor and say, "Pastor, we really need to do this ministry well. I will do everything I can to show good stewardship and help with fundraising, but we are going to need finances to make this happen."

If you are going to build a youth ministry, you have to make an investment in it. It will take money to provide good facilities. It will take money for promotion and advertising. Finances are necessary for outreach to be effective. So have an honest conversation with your pastor.

Let him know, "I understand there are many expectations from the different departments in the church who all need money to do their ministries, but we can't afford to ignore and possibly lose our young people."

If you are a Senior Pastor, please look at the words of Jesus. In John 21:15 Jesus said to Peter, "Peter, do you love me?"

And Peter said, "Yes, I love you."

And Jesus said, "Feed my lambs." And then He said a second time, "Do you love me?"

And Peter a second time said, "Yes, Lord, I love you."

Jesus said, "Feed my sheep." And then the third time He said, "Peter do you love me?"

And Peter said, "Yes, I love you, Lord."

And He said, "Feed my sheep."

Notice, the first response from Jesus was, "Feed my lambs." Go after the young people. Peter's first priority as the leader and pastor of the church of Jerusalem was to go after the young. I believe at least one third of our church budgets should be allocated for our children and young people.

You must make a significant contribution and commitment to reach young people with the resources of your church. They are a mission field. It is almost like a part of our missions budget. We must reach that mission field of youth culture that has not been reached, and it takes money to do it.

When Pastor George first made the commitment to reach the young people of our church with Oneighty®, and then, ultimately, the young people of our community through the Oneighty® program, we initially invested tens of thousands of dollars into our facilities alone. That included the cost to redo our walls, lighting, backdrop, sound, and staging. That was to accommodate a couple hundred young people. Maybe your church is smaller and you don't have to make that size of an investment initially, but it's going to take something significant to get the job done right.

Matthew 6:21 says, "Where your treasure is, there your heart will be also." And if your heart and the heart of your church is really to reach the young people of your church and community, then where your heart is, your treasure will be. You will make the financial commitment.

Begin to place demands in that area and believe God. As a youth pastor, place demands on your workers and students. In your weekly offerings say, "Let's make a commitment to this."

We bought our Oneighty® mobile, our 1934 Ford hot-rod, to provide incentive for our kids to bring friends to our services each week. If they bring eight visitors to Oneighty®, over any length of time, we give them a ride home from school in the hot-rod. We discussed this earlier in the book.

We put that vision out before our kids and said, "Hey, we want to see this car become a part of our ministry." We showed them a picture of it, and then we said, "We're going to let you raise some money for this." Our students, through offerings and fund raisers, gave cheerfully and raised extra money to help meet the needs to buy that car. We were able to buy it with the sacrifices of our students.

We recently started a stewardship campaign in our church to build a brand new facility, currently under construction. It is a 90-thousand square foot youth facility on 35 acres of land, surrounded by recreation of every kind. This is a huge project, costing millions of dollars. We went to our own students and said, "Over the next year and a half, as we build this Oneighty® facility, we want you to give toward this." They pledged $148,000 dollars over 18 months, above their tithes each week. They began to give, some $5 a week, some $10 a week, some $2 a week.

God will use your young people and your workers to help meet the needs of your ministry. It takes significant financial commitment to build your ministry. Place a demand to see that commitment met.

Demandment Number 6: I Will Execute Change.

The next demand you must place upon your ministry is the demand of proper protocol to make significant changes in your ministry. In order to grow your ministry and reach the next level, you have to make changes. That's a given.

If you go back to the old leadership strategy and keep doing what you have always done, you will continue to have what you have always had. If you want to do new things, make improvements and grow, there must be changes to make it happen. The key is making those changes well.

Changes made the wrong way can bring disaster. Changes made the right way can produce ongoing fruit and success. You must realize there is proper protocol for change.

Good change is like gravity; it must make its way down. Successful change cannot start at the bottom of the authority ladder. It requires change at the top and gradually moves that change down.

Proverbs 15:22 says, "Without counsel, plans go awry, but in the multitude of counsel, they are established." Plans are things you want to change. If you have a plan, you are going to do something that will bring about change. You don't plan to do something you are already doing or something that's already been accomplished. You plan things that you haven't done. A plan in its very nature is change. We could insert the word *plans* for *change* there.

So let's read it that way. "Without counsel, change goes awry, but in a multitude of counsel, change becomes established." We must solicit counsel from those in leadership in order to make sure our change is strongly established.

Starting at the top, there are eight channels you need to go through when making a change.

Number one: all change goes through the ultimate authority, God, and the head of the Church, Jesus Christ. Never launch any kind of change until you submit it to God. Talk to God about it. Say, "Lord, is this something we need to do?"

We have given you many ideas, and I caution you not to do everything you see in a book or hear on tape. For every model you follow and everyone you look to, take whatever you're thinking about implementing into your ministry and submit it to God. Nine times out of ten you're going to want to take action. Even as you use ideas and strategies from this book, be sensitive to the Holy Spirit in your timing. You may have a sense of witness in your heart, *This is right. I feel good about this.*

Always run things by the Lord and submit your changes to His Word. God speaks through His Word. Make sure the changes you are implementing line up with the Word of God. God is your first authority channel.

Number two: submit changes to your pastor. Run any change you do through your pastor. Submit your changes, especially major, significant ones, to him. "Pastor, what do you think about remodeling our facility," or "I'm looking at changing some of our leadership structure with my key leaders. What do you think? I'm going to take this person out and put this person in. Do you have any observations?" Submit your changes to your pastor.

Number three: submit changes to your staff. If you are a full-time paid youth pastor and you have an assistant, secretary, or several people on your staff, submit the changes to them.

I am not saying you should ask them to tell you what to do, but get their input. Make sure you establish that change well. They may see some things that will help you better implement that change and give you wise counsel.

Number four: submit changes to your senior department leaders. Meet with all those in leadership in your youth ministry first. This would include your head ushers, music and worship leaders, altar counseling leaders, and maybe your campus ministry leader, if you have one. Discuss all your changes with them and say, "Hey, this is where we're going. This is what we are doing, and I want to get your input. What do you think about this?"

Number five: meet with all your workers. You are announcing change. Therefore, all your key department leaders, staff, if you have them, plus all your other workers need to be informed of the change. At that point you're not really looking for them to give you ideas or suggestions, but you're announcing the direction you are going and how you're going to make it happen, and they need to know about it first, before you announce it to the students. They need to feel like they are on the inside track.

That is important. People want to be on the inside track. Your workers will feel they are included.

Number six: talk to your students. On your meeting night with all your teenagers announce this new change, "Hey, everyone, we're building a brand new facility. We are getting ready to totally remodel. It will be done in such and such a time, and we want you to be part of it. We're going to have some work nights, and you can come out and help." Really build it up, and preach the vision. Announce it to your students.

Number seven: announce it to the community. Submit press releases about your new facility or outreach. Let others know through advertisement on radio and send post-cards to the whole mailing list. Again, make sure your students know before you do that. They should not hear about some new thing you are doing through the radio. Honor your students.

Number eight: the last person to know is the devil. Tell the devil, "Devil, we don't care what you say, what you think, or how you're going to try to stop us. We don't care what you are going to try to do to hinder this new plan; you're not going to make it happen. We are going forward. We have our faces set like a flint. We are not going to stop until we see this vision fulfilled and accomplished. We want you to know it will succeed. There is nothing you can do to stop us. "If God be for us, no one can be against us" (Rom. 8:31).

This is how you cascade change effectively. If you will observe this process, you eliminate the risk of a bad experience. By doing this you will build an alliance that will both protect you and propel you toward your goals in ministry. Make sure you walk through these channels, implementing change correctly.

Demandment Number 7: I Will Release My Faith.

Demand a spirit of faith in all you set out to achieve. This is an important demand you must place on yourself and your people. It is the demand of faith. If you are going to grow a ministry, you have to have a spirit of faith. You must believe strongly in where you are going and in what you are doing. Faith comes by speaking the Word of God over your ministry.

And faith comes by hearing, and hearing by the Word of God (Romans 10:17).

You must bring people on board, proclaim your vision, and stir up their faith for where you are going. Tell them what is going to happen.

Hebrews 11:1 says, "Now faith is the substance of the things that are hoped for, the evidence of things not seen." When you have things that you're hoping for, or things in the future that aren't seen yet, believe in those things before they ever become substance, something you can actually touch.

It starts with you. You have to believe you can reach hundreds of students in your community. You must know God will supply your finances.

You can't walk around thinking, *Well, I wonder if this is gonna happen. Boy, I sure hope kids will come to this youth group. Boy, I don't know if this is really gonna grow or not. We'll see.*

You cannot have that kind of attitude. You must operate in a spirit of faith as a leader, and put a spirit of faith into your leaders and your students through the Word of God. Tell them, "We're going to see this happen. This is something God wants to do."

He wants to grow your ministry even more than you want to grow it. He wants to reach the lost. Jesus paid the price and shed His blood so sinners could be reached. He wants to bring as many young people into your youth group as possible.

God is on board with you. He wants to make it happen. He wants to help you disciple these kids.

The Bible also says, in Hebrews 11:6, "Without faith, it is impossible to please [God]: for he that cometh to God must believe that he is, and that he is a rewarder of them that diligently seek him."

If you don't have a spirit of faith and believe in things before you see them, you can't please God. When you come to God, you can't just believe that He is God. You also need to believe He is a rewarder.

God wants to reward you. You are working hard in ministry and serving Him with everything you have. You have made sacrifices. He is a good God and wants to help you grow. He desires to give you good leaders, good facilities, and bless your finances. He wants to give you resources, such as buses and vans. He wants to bless you in every area of your ministry.

Believe that! Accept it! Embrace it and pass that message of faith and optimism to your workers and leaders. Let them know God is going to build this ministry, and it will grow.

I remember years ago at Oneighty® God gave me a plan and a vision to fill the largest convention center in our city with a See-You-After-The-Pole Rally. Most of you have participated in See-You-At-The-Pole, where students meet together at their flag poles the third Wednesday morning of every September and pray for our communities, cities, and schools. We decided to do a huge See-You-After-The-Pole Rally, and God spoke to me about using the Oral Roberts University Mabee Center, which seats about 7,500 students.

At the time, we were running about 900 to 1,000 students in our weekly services. God gave me the vision, and I talked to my pastor about it. He said, "Blaine, that's right. I bear witness to that and we need to do it."

I remember getting up in front of our students. We had 1,000 kids and we were telling them we were going to fill the Mabee Center. God spoke to my heart, and I gave them a spirit of faith. I said, "We're going to reach our friends and fill up that center with 7,500 young people. We're trusting and believing God for 1,000 students to make commitments to Christ that night."

I put out that vision. I showed them in the Word of God how God wants all sinners to come to repentance, and we prayed for that. We believed God together, as a church and as a youth ministry, for 7,500 young people to show up that night.

We asked God to give us the steps to take, and God showed us how to see that vision become a reality. He showed us how to market, advertise, and promote it. He directed us in how to sell tickets at the right price, and how to have the right things at that event that would draw the kids in. We invited the right guests.

Two days before the event happened, we completely sold out of tickets. That night we had 7,500 young people in attendance. It was packed to the ceiling. There was such an excitement, energy, and anticipation.

We delivered the program, had worship and praise, and preached. We held a short concert, a drama skit, and a video. It was a powerful evening. As we gave the call for salvation, more than 2,000 students came forward and gave their lives to Christ.

In the very beginning as I shared the vision with our kids, there were doubts that flew through my mind. Those doubts said, You'll be lucky to have 1,500 kids there. You'll be lucky to have 2,000.

Faith is not an absence of doubts in your mind. Faith says, *I'm going to cast out these doubts, as much as they're attacking me. I refuse to listen to them and I refuse to speak them.* Faith says, *I am determined to speak the Word of God. I choose to believe what God says, and what God has spoken to me.*

As you grow and as God gives you a vision for your ministry, you might have doubters and skeptics. Doubts may come to your own mind, but don't allow those doubts to come out of your mouth. Speak with a spirit of faith. Speak your vision, and go for the things that God has put in your heart. Your vision and faith will one day have evidence and substance.

Demandment Number 8: I Will Outlast the Critics.

The next demand you have to place on your ministry, as you build and construct a successful ministry, is a proper response to criticism. As you do these demands to build a strong ministry, you will grow and have a successful, fruitful ministry.

Unfortunately, there will be critics along the way. I can honestly say that in 20 years of youth ministry, I have had more criticism in the last six years than ever before. Yet, I have also had more success in reaching students for Christ in the last six years than ever before.

It seems like the more success we have, the more souls we win, the more kids we take on mission trips, the more we grow, the more critics come out.

It was like that in Jesus' ministry. He was criticized in great measure by Pharisees, the religious people who thought they knew more than He did. They were envious of the results and the crowds that followed Him. As you grow, you will experience criticism. The key is to respond to criticism in the right way.

There are three kinds of criticism you will experience: true, half-truth, and false.

When you have criticism that is true, right, and just, make the appropriate changes. I remember as we began to have large numbers of kids come to Oneighty®, our facility became overwhelmed with students. I had a parent call and ask to meet with me. She said, "Blaine, I love what you are doing, but I have one criticism." She said, "Your game room is overrun with kids before and after the services. You don't have enough workers in there, and things are happening that are not good. I couldn't find my kid the other night, kids were abusing some of the games, kids were bullying other kids and saying things they shouldn't say. You probably need more workers in there."

Therefore, I went through the game room the next Wednesday night, and I noticed we didn't have enough workers in there. I thanked that parent. I said, "Thanks for watching out for my back. I hadn't seen that."

We made the changes. Now I have monitors in every section of the game room, and they work to help the parents coming in to pick up their kids. The monitors make sure there is control and discipline, and the kids are not abusing games or each other. That helped me. When you experience constructive criticism, make the changes that will help you grow.

Second, you will experience criticism that is half-true. They will say things about what you are doing, but the criticism of those things is not right. I've had people criticize us and say things like, "Well, the only reason kids come is because you have games at Oneighty®, or you give away free food from time to time."

And granted, some kids come because of the games, but that is not true across the board. Although some kids do come only for the games initially, eventually many come to Christ and begin to serve Jesus as they hear the Word of God in a service. They become disciples and go through our eight-week discipleship program. They find themselves serving God on a mission trip one day.

It is really a half-truth. When you have criticism like that, it is important to stand on the Word of God in what you are doing. Make sure what you are doing is based on principles in the Word of God. One of the reasons we have games and food is because Jesus wants us to meet the needs of kids on all three levels—spirit, soul, and body.

In 1 Corinthians 5:23, Paul prayed we would be whole in our spirit, soul, and body. There is nothing wrong with the social and physical aspect of life. You can have a wholesome social life while enjoying good relationships as part of the body of Christ.

Jesus said, "Follow me, and I'll make you fishers of men." (Matt. 4:19.) If you are a good fisherman, you will have good bait on your hook, and you will draw those fish in. Make sure you stand on the Word of God with the things you are doing, and pronounce and proclaim that. Help your young people, leaders, and workers understand why you do the things you do. Everything we do is based on principles in the Word of God.

Third, you will experience false criticism. It is simply not true. A fairly well-known evangelist was telling people about a particular youth group who used numbers in their name. He said they were bringing students to the altar, then taking these students to a dark room and forcing them to speak in other tongues. He did not name us, but gave enough information so people could figure out who he was talking about. This criticism got back to me.

Obviously, it was not true. We would never do anything like that. It was completely, false. It had never happened and would never happen. I had to respond.

The best way to respond to criticism like that is to respond directly to the person from whom the criticism has come; do it in a spirit of love, but at the same time, let them know that it is wrong. You can't just ignore it because that person could damage your credibility, your reputation, and the ministry.

I called the evangelist on the phone. It took me awhile to find his number, but I got it. First, I asked him if what I heard he was saying was true. He said, "Yes, I have been saying that. But that's what I heard you were doing. And I don't think that's right."

I said, "Sir, you should have called me directly. You should have made sure your source was accurate. I am here to tell you it is not true. I ask that you go back to every pastor, either by phone or face-to-face, and tell them what you said was not true, and repair the damage you have created with your misinformation. Let them know you were wrong and that we do not do that." He repented to his credit. He agreed to make restitution, and saved us from further undue attacks on our reputation and ministry.

Don't allow Satan to use people to destroy your ministry. When you hear of things, approach the person or people without anger. Don't accuse them, but say, "I want to talk to you about this. Is it true you were saying this?"

There have been other local church youth pastors in our city who accused us of stealing their sheep. I am very proactive with that one. I call that youth pastor, talk to him on the phone, or meet him for lunch, and say, "Hey, listen, I heard you've been upset with us, or critical because you think we're stealing your kids. Is that true?" I assure you we are not stealing their sheep. I tell them, "We are believing God for you to grow. In fact, I will help you grow. Come to Oneighty®. Maybe there are some methods or ideas you could use in your ministry."

We have actually done that. We have had approximately twelve different churches, pastors, and youth pastors from our city come to Oneighty® to learn from us and see what we are doing. They have gone through our seminars, and we have spent time with them individually. They have gone back, grown, and learned how to reach and disciple teenagers.

We don't allow division like that to happen in our city, but we reach out, and we ask them, "Hey, are you saying those things, or do you feel threatened in any ways." And in most cases, they've been honest and said, "Yeah, I have said those things, or I have felt those feelings, and I've expressed those feelings to other people."

We've been proactive and said, "Hey, we're going after unchurched kids." I've told them, "If you ever hear of or know of one of my workers trying to pull one of your kids to our group, you let me know about it, and we'll take care of it."

I've also been proactive with our students and our leaders. At our next leadership meeting, I let our students and our leaders know, "Hey, we're not trying to reach other churches' kids. Let's go after kids that don't have churches."

When you have criticism that is false, go to those sources and deal with them directly. The Bible tells us to "speak the truth in love..." (Eph. 4:15). You will find that you will win people to your cause.

The Bible says in Proverbs 28:23, "He who rebukes a man, will find more favor afterward than he who flatters with the tongue." I believe it is important for you to confront an issue like this rather than ignore it. The Bible says that if you rebuke, eventually you will find a friend.

Demandment Number 9: I Will Grow Personally.

The next demand you have to do as you build and construct a growing youth ministry is a demand upon yourself and your team to stay edified and educated, and to evaluate. Let's deal with these one at a time.

You must constantly keep yourself and your team edified to make sure you continue to grow. Take steps to ensure that you don't burn out by getting so busy and working so hard that you become weary or tired.

As you develop a ministry and it takes off, it becomes a lot of work. There are times you have to sow into it in order to maintain a growing ministry. You and your workers have to pay the price, make sacrifices, and work hard.

It's easy to want to quit, if you don't stay edified, even when you are succeeding. It is not enough to climb the mountain and get to the top, but you want to stay on top. You want to stay successful and maintain your growth.

I am so proud of our team at Oneighty®. We have not just built a large youth ministry, but we have maintained a large and growing youth ministry. It is in its sixth year now, and we are still growing and developing. We are not losing ground. In order to do that, we have to stay edified.

You and your workers can stay edified when good, strong, personal friendships are maintained. We all need good people speaking into our life and encouraging us.

You need to be in church every week. Do not become so busy that you are not sitting under your pastor and the Word of God. Continually allow the Word, praise, and worship to feed your spirit and keep you built up.

Watch your words, and encourage your leaders and workers to watch their words. Negative and pessimistic words can destroy you. "I am full of stress. I am burnt out. I am full of anxiety. I don't know if I'm gonna make it." Don't allow those words to come out of your mouth. Even if you are thinking those thoughts, do not speak those words.

Don't speak things contrary to what you know to be true from the Word of God. The Bible says your words, or your tongue, is like a rudder, and it has the ability to direct even great ships. (James 3:4,5). Your words determine your direction.

If you talk negatively and speak defeat, that is where your life is headed, and ultimately, that is where your ministry will end up. Speak where you want to go. Speak faith, joy, and encouragement even if you are discouraged and depressed. "Thank You, Lord, that I'm encouraged, that You're greater in me than he that's in the world, and that I can do all things through Christ who strengthens me." Then encourage your workers to speak the Word of God over their life and the ministry as well.

The second personal demand is education. As you continue to grow, you must continue to learn. I am a learner and I never stop learning. I go to seminars, read new books, and listen to new audiotapes. I stay on a learning curve.

Encourage your leaders and workers to stay in school! Take your team to leadership training seminars, conferences, and conventions annually, at the least. Keep them learning and growing. You can read books, listen to tapes, and pass them on to your leaders. Have a regular training time for your workers where you bring them together, train them, and encourage them.

We have a program every month called *Thrive.* It is a leadership-training program for youth pastors, but it is also a program where youth pastors can receive training and pass it on to their leaders. Tools and resources are critical. Continually educate yourself and your leaders.

Then there is evaluation. From time to time, you need to go back and ask yourself, "Am I reaching the goals we've set out to accomplish?" Ask your leaders if they are achieving the goals they set out to accomplish in their departments. Are you growing your team? Are you seeing new leaders and workers come into the fold? Ask yourself, "Are we continuing to grow our leadership base?"

Then ask yourself, "What kind of people are we growing with? Are we attracting good, quality leaders? "Remember, the leaders you have over your ministry will never attract a stronger leader than the ones they are.

If you rated your leaders on a scale of one to ten and you had a leader who rated a six, that person is not a great leader. They lack in some leadership skills. Maybe they are a little bit disorganized or do not know how to communicate well. They are faithful and have good character, but as far as their influence, they may be a six on the leader scale.

If you put a six leader in a department, that leader will attract fives and fours, in terms of leadership ability. As you look at your leadership team, I encourage you to make sure you have eights and nines or nines and tens in your key areas of leadership. Then you will attract eights, sevens, and sixes, who are good workers to serve under them.

From time to time, evaluate your department leaders. Ask yourself, "Do I have eights? Do I have nines or tens in my key departments?" Maybe you have had some fives or a sixes, who are not producing like they could. Become willing to go back and make a change there. You could move them into another area of ministry, like helping or assisting rather than being a key leader.

In the evaluation process, ask those you really trust, maybe your spouse, a key leader, or an associate on your staff, to give you an evaluation. "I'm seeing the ministry from my perspective, but tell me what you see. How can we do better? How can we grow? How can I do better as youth pastor, or youth leader? What can I do to construct a better program?"

If you ask for honesty, and you're careful to say, "Hey, don't be mean to me, but tell me the truth. What can we do?" you will receive an honest evaluation that will help you improve and grow.

Those areas are going to be critical to you as you maintain your ministry, edify, educate, and evaluate in order to maintain your growth.

Demandment Number 10: I Will Lead My Home.

The last demand, and maybe the most important demand that you have to place upon yourself in order to have a long-term growing ministry, is the demand of personal responsibility, in your own life and toward your spouse and children.

I am talking to those who are married, and perhaps those who have children. If you are not married right now, or you don't have kids right now, go ahead and read this section because it will help prepare you for the days ahead. Preparation is a good thing.

A good home life is a requirement. One of the qualifications of an overseer or elder is, "You must rule well your own house, having your children in all gravity..." (1 Tim 3:4). That means they're not climbing the walls, but they are under control and you have a good home life.

Without a good home life, your ministry will suffer. You must really work at your home. I encourage you to never let ministry become so busy that you neglect your wife, husband, or children.

Speaking of the wife, the Bible says:

> Husbands likewise, dwell with them with understanding, giving honor to the wife, as to the weaker vessel, as being heirs together of the grace of life, that your prayers may not be hindered (1 Peter 3:7).

God asks us to have understanding in order to do well in our marriages. I believe we have to have an understanding in our marriages in order to have success.

First, understand a poor marriage will hinder your ministry from successfulness. The Bible says, literally, that your prayers will not be answered if you don't understand how to honor your wife or husband. The things you are praying for in your ministry and in your personal life will be stopped. You don't want that hindrance, so instead, build on a foundation that is good, and build a ministry together that will last a long time.

Understand your spouse's desire to contribute in ministry with his or her unique gifting. You will have to find the right plan and the right way for your spouse to be part of your ministry. Don't put your spouse into a box and say, "You've gotta do this, or you've gotta do that, because this person over here does it this way."

When I first entered ministry, I was with a pastor in Canada whose wife was extremely involved in ministry. She taught and was responsible for certain areas of the ministry in the church. My model of a pastor's wife at that time was for her to be very involved.

My wife didn't like to do that. She didn't want to be over certain areas. She didn't like to preach and to teach, and we had to work through that and discover the best way for my wife, Cathy, to contribute.

I began to find out her unique gifting was not organizing a ministry, or speaking from the pulpit, but it was helping me by coming to church on Wednesday nights, when I was doing youth, and being there to interact with leaders. She spoke into their lives and was a friend to the girls in the youth ministry. She is better one-on-one than I am, and so she is able to spend time with people and do things I am not able to do. Allow your spouse to find their unique way of contributing with their gifts.

Next, you must understand your spouse has a need to be the first one to know the most important things in your life. You don't want your spouse to find out about a major new thing you are doing in your youth ministry through someone else. Communicate with your spouse.

"Honey, this is what's happening in Oneighty®, and this is where we're going. We are going to build a brand new facility, and we are doing a missions trip to Africa." Let your spouse know about things you are doing, before you begin to tell everyone else.

Understand the importance in marriage of continuing to romance and date each other. Keep romance alive in your marriage. Romance is doing special things that are out of the ordinary, such as calling her during the day for no apparent reason and saying, "Honey, I love you." Bring home flowers when it is not your anniversary or her birthday. Put a postcard or a letter in the mail to her listing "all the reasons why I married you, and why I am still so glad I am married to you." Have a date night.

Cathy and I try to have a date night alone about once a week. It doesn't have to be expensive. You can have coffee together or go to a movie, as long as you spend time together talking about family, life, ministry, and your future. Keep romance and dating alive.

Understand the differences that exist between a man and a woman. Remember you and your spouse are different and have different needs. Learning to respect those differences early on will help you grow together.

Understand, guys, that if you are working in the office all day, when you get home your wife needs to talk to you. Although you've spilled out your 20,000 words a day, maybe she still has 10 to 15,000 she needs to get out before the evening ends. You can't come home and put a newspaper in your face, turn the TV on, and expect to have a good marriage. You have to spend some time each evening talking about the day.

Remember that marriage is give and take. A good marriage is learning to give and make sacrifices. That's what love is. Love says, *I want the best for the other person, not myself.* So, make those sacrifices together.

Understand the benefits of your union together. The Bible says that when you come together as husband and wife, you are one and that unity brings power in the things you do together. (Eccl. 4:12.) You have so many wonderful advantages in being a husband or wife. (Eph. 5:31.)

One of the greatest advantages I have with my wonderful wife is that she will be honest with me. Cathy will tell me when I am missing it, when I have a bad attitude, or if I have become a little bit arrogant. She loves me enough to approach me and let me know those things. You need a pride buster—someone who will save you from a fall. Your spouse can save you from embarrassment because he or she can see things you need to know about before someone else finds out, such as a character flaw. That is a wonderful benefit.

Your wife or husband can give you perspective on decisions you have to make that only he or she can see. Many times my wife has seen things in certain leaders I had not seen, a red flag I needed to watch and wasn't aware of. They might have discernment that you don't have.

They can be supportive in times when the enemy attacks you, or when you go through a trying circumstance in your church or ministry and you feel like quitting. That spouse may be the only person who keeps you centered, encouraged, and built up.

Then there is strength to the tenth power that you have together. The Bible says one will put a thousand to flight, but two, ten thousand. (Deut. 32:30.) There is a tenth power strength that together you should rely on God for. As you come together in prayer, unified vision, and service in ministry, you will accomplish ten times as much than if you try to do it alone.

Don't let this be just your ministry, but a ministry you are in together. If you will do these things, and commit to these things together, you will have a ministry that will last and last. It will be long term, and you will not allow your lives, your marriage, or your ministry to shipwreck down the road.

Understand the need for your children to have a Dad and Mom, not a pastor. It is important to spend time with your kids, not just as the pastor, but as Dad or Mom. You need to give them instruction in the Word and raise them as godly children. It is not enough for my kids to hear the Word of God when I preach it on Wednesday nights.

I have three boys. Two are teenagers and one is almost a teenager, and I'm their youth pastor. I preach to them every Wednesday night. Someone asked, "Blaine, how do you develop your messages every week?" I figure out what my kids are doing wrong, and that is what I preach on that week, and if anyone else gets blessed, great.

I get the chance to preach to my own kids every week, but I also spend time with them on a personal basis, as Dad. I talk to them about what it means to be a Christian, how to serve God and follow Christ. We have Bible studies and pray together regularly. That must happen; it can't just be at church.

I make sure the church and the youth ministry do not become the enemy of my kids by allowing it to steal all my personal time. I do not allow myself to be gone every night of the week. If I am gone every weekend, I can't take my kids to a movie. I can't spend time with them in the evening laughing, having fun, eating popcorn together, playing in the backyard, throwing the football around, and just being a dad.

We make sure we don't become too busy in ministry. That means prioritizing. I can't get to some things every week. I can't do everything I want to do in ministry. But I'd rather have my family and my kids grow up loving and serving God, than to lose my kids and gain a great youth ministry.

I make sure I take my days off and have evenings to spend time with them. That keeps them from ever resenting the church or ministry.

I never ask my kids to behave in certain ways just because they are the youth pastor's kids. I'll never sit down with my middle son, Dillon, and say, "Hey, Dillon, you know you've got to behave in this area, because if you don't it'll look bad on me, since I'm the youth pastor and people know you're my kid." I will never do that. That is completely irresponsible and unnecessary. It is something you never want to put on your child.

When I have asked my kids to elevate to certain standards of behavior in their personal life—how they treat people, their relationships with the opposite sex, their language, or their entertainment—it is never because they are pastor's kids. It is because they are Christians. It is because this is what the Word of God says, and we open the Scripture together. We say, "This is what the Bible says and this is why we have these standards, and this is why you need to live this way." I tell them, "These things that I'm asking of you are the same things I would ask of you if I was just a Christian father, serving in a secular occupation. This is because you want to please Christ, not because you are a pastor's kid."

Again, that will stop them from resenting the ministry.

Protect your ministry, and as you follow all of these demandments and place them on yourself, your ministry, and your church, you will have a growing ministry.

We talked about a lot of time-honored rules in this book that you need to break in order to grow, and in this final chapter, we discussed ten demands you will want to keep to have success. I believe, as you put these things into practice one step at a time and prioritize your steps, God will help you grow.

The Bible says, "The steps of the righteous man are ordered of the Lord" (Ps. 37:23). Right now, allow God to give you every step you need to see your ministry begin to grow, and to reach more and more teenagers. As you grow your ministry and develop your outreaches, you never know what is going to happen in these young people.

Through 20 years of ministry, I have had the chance to see some of our young people grow up and develop their lives. The Bible says our children are like arrows, and as we send them out from the bow of the local church, and the bow of youth ministry, they will find their mark. (Ps. 127:4.) Once we release these young people from student ministry into adult life and they begin to serve God, God begins to help that arrow find its place. We don't always know exactly where they will go or what they will do, but we will be amazed to see where they're going.

Some of the kids in your ministry who may seem awkward and the least likely to do something great for God, will be some of the greatest trophies and treasures you have in the days to come.

Ten years ago there was a skinny little kid in our youth group who quietly went about his business serving God. He wasn't a big "rah-rah!" Christian, but was solid and committed. His name was Whitney. Today we call him Whit and he's my chief creative consultant at Oneighty® and our lead worship leader. Whit designed our Oneighty® logo and does most of our major brochures. He's an arrow that found its mark!

In fact, most of our Oneighty® staff team are a wonderful collection of young people who grew up in our children's and youth ministry and are now some of our best employees. We spent a lot of time, money, and energy investing in these kids and now they're investing in us. Youth ministry doesn't cost you; it pays!

Years ago there was a 13-year-old young man who came to our youth group faithfully every week. His name was Hugh. He won't mind me telling you that he wasn't the most popular kid in our group. It's not that he didn't have any friends, but he wasn't the kind of young person who stood out in a crowd. One day at church Hugh shared something with me that God had put on his heart. I looked at him with a curious anticipation. "What is it?" I asked him.

He said, "Blaine, I believe God has called me to be the president of the United States one day."

I looked at him and thought, *My goodness. I don't think that's ever going to happen. This guy would have trouble getting elected by his own peers, in this youth group, never mind by a country. I just don't see a lot of leadership ability in this kid. I sure don't see him becoming president.*

I couldn't tell him that. I didn't want to discourage him, so I told him I was proud of his aspirations and that I would pray for him. I did pray for Hugh. He needed it. His home life had its share of troubles and he was going to need God's help to make it.

"Lord," I prayed, "help direct Hugh, and help his life become a success. Make him a great leader, and Lord, the Bible says, "All things are possible," even if they are highly unlikely I thank You, Lord, that You can raise up Hugh one day to be president if it's Your will. Lord, make him a great leader, and if he is called to be president, then I thank You that he will do that. In Jesus' name, amen."

Shortly after that Cathy and I began to travel in ministry, and later we moved to Colorado to pastor for a time.

One day as I was walking through a mall, a young man walked up to me and said, "Hey, you're Blaine Bartel."

I looked back at him and said, "And, who are you?"

It was Hugh. I hadn't seen Hugh for over ten years. He was college age now. I didn't realize it until I started talking to him, and he said, "Blaine, how are you doing?"

I said, "Well, I'm doing great. How are you doing?"

He said, "Blaine, God has blessed me so much. God is showing me how to be a leader."

And I said, "Tell me about it."

He said, "Well, I'm just about to graduate from Tulsa University and I am the student body president for the whole school."

I said, "You've gotta be kidding. That's great!"

He said, "That's not all. I'm also the president of the College Republicans here at the university."

I said, "Hugh, that's wonderful."

He said, "The Lord's also graced me to sit on more than 20 different boards in the school and in the city of Tulsa. He's taught me how to influence, lead, and negotiate with other people. I've had the opportunity to serve as an intern for one of the senators from our state."

Then he looked at me and said, "Blaine, I think I told you, but I'm on my way to becoming president of the United States."

This time, I looked back at him and said, "Hugh, we gotta stay in touch, man. It has been too long. I believe you're gonna do it." I saw a young man who, at 13 years old, had a pastor, a youth pastor, a mom, and a stepfather who encouraged him to pray, to dream dreams, and to believe that God could do great things in his life.

A young man heard the Word of God and learned how to apply it in his life. A young man who was learning how to be a great leader took what he'd learned in his youth group, church, and family and moved out of the bow of that youth ministry to be an arrow that would hit his mark in the world. I just had lunch with Hugh last week. He is now 25 years old. He's still actively working and preparing himself to be a great leader in our nation. Will he ever be president? Maybe, maybe not. But it won't surprise me if he does. Will he be a great leader and influence people for good? He is already doing that.

I want you to know that as you send these arrows out of your youth ministry, they will fly to places you never dreamed they would go. They will hit marks and achieve things you never thought they could achieve. As you reach these kids every week—as you pray for them, as you love them, as you prepare for them—realize every bit of work, every bit of sweat, every prayer you pray is for a reason. You're helping mold destiny, changing lives and ultimately changing your world.

Thank you for making the sacrifice and paying the price to love this generation. Heaven sees your work and effort. Don't ever forget it. God bless you and your ministry.

THE "TEN DEMANDMENTS"

1. I WILL BE LOYAL.
2. I WILL BUILD MY CORE.
3. I WILL ALTER OUR IMAGE.
4. I WILL LAUNCH.
5. I WILL INVEST.
6. I WILL EXECUTE CHANGE.
7. I WILL RELEASE MY FAITH.
8. I WILL OUTLAST THE CRITICS.
9. I WILL GROW PERSONALLY.
10. I WILL LEAD MY HOME.

turn life

While many, if not most of you, who are reading this book have made a decision to make Jesus Christ your Lord, perhaps you are one who has not. I would love to help you if you are not sure of your salvation.

The decision to follow Jesus Christ is much more than "turning over a new leaf" or trying to live a better life. It is asking God to give you a brand new heart. If the heart or spirit of a person can be changed, outward actions and ambitions will follow.

The Bible describes this supernatural work in a human life as being born again. In the book of John, chapter 3, there was a very religious man named Nicodemus. If you are unfamiliar with the Bible, look up the starting page number for the book of John in the table of contents. He asked Jesus how he could be guaranteed eternal life. Jesus did not tell him to be a better person, walk old ladies across the street, or even attend church at least once a week. He told Nicodemus he must be born again.

This was not a physical rebirth, but rather a spiritual one. When you ask Christ into your life, He promises to give you a brand new spirit and make you a brand new person. On the outside, everything may look and even feel the same, but on the inside you have been given a new heart.

Paul, a leader among the very first Christians, sent a letter to the Christians in the city of Corinth, Greece, about what it means to be born again. "Therefore, if anyone is in Christ, he is a new creation: old things have passed away: behold, all things have become new" (2 Cor. 5:17).

Why not pray this prayer with me right now?

Heavenly Father, thank You for sending Your Son Jesus to be the sacrifice for my sins. Right now, I boldly confess Jesus as the Lord and Master of my life. I believe He rose from the dead, and I receive the free gift of eternal life. Thank You for giving me a new heart and the opportunity to be born again. In Jesus' name, Amen.

Now let me encourage you to continue in these four things:

1. Read the Bible daily.

2. Pray every day.

3. Attend a good, Bible-teaching church.

4. Share your faith in Christ with others.

> May God's best be yours always!
> Serving America's Future,
> *Blaine Bartel*

endnotes

Chapter 1
[1] Rainer, p. 3.
[2] Rainer, p. 169.
[3] Rainer, p. 5.
[4] See note 2 above.
[5] Rainer, p. 6.
[6] See note 2 above.
[7] Rainer, p. 2.
[8] See note 2 above.
[9] *Campus Life.*
[10] Ibid.

Chapter 2
[1] Vine, s.v. "young," p. 692.
[2] Vine, s.v. "elder," p. 195.
[3] Barna.
[4] *World Christian Encyclopedia.*
[5] Collins.

Chapter 4
[1] Robbins.

Chapter 7
[1] Dawn Ministries.

Chapter 8
[1] *Plugged In.*
[2] McDowell.
[3] Barna.

Chapter 9
[1] Shaw, line 124.

Chapter 12
[1] Maxwell.

references

Barna, George, Barna Research Group, Ltd. 5528 Everglades Street, Ventura, California. (805) 658-8885. http://www.barna.org

Barrett, David B., George T. Kurian and Todd M. Johnson, *World Christian Encyclopedia.* New York: Oxford University Press, 2001.

Campus Life, Carol Stream, Illinois: Christianity Today International, 1994-2001. www.christianity.com/teens

Collins, James C. and Jerry I. Porras, *Built to Last.* New York: HarperCollins Publishers, 1997.

Dawn Ministries, Colorado Springs, Colorado.

Josh McDowell Ministry, P.O. Box 131000, Dallas, Texas. (972) 907-1000. http://www.josh.org/

Maxwell, John, "Injoy Life Club" leadership lesson entitled, "Keep On Keeping On...Consistency" Vol. 9, No. 7.

Plugged In, published by Focus on the Family, Colorado Springs, Colorado. (800) 232-6459. http://www.fotf.org/

Rainer, Thom S., *The Bridger Generation.* Nashville: Broadman & Holman Publishers, 1997.

Robbins, Anthony, *Unlimited Power.* Simon and Schuster Audio,01/2000.

Shaw, Bernard, *Man and Superman.* Cambridge: The University Press, 1903. New York: Bartleby.com, 1999. http://www.bartleby.com/157/

Vine, W.E., *Vine's Complete Expository Dictionary of Old and New Testament Words.* Nashville: Thomas Nelson, 1996.

illustrations

Chapter 6

"The Oneighty® Organization" from "Breaking the Law, Blaine's Teaching Outlines," Session 2, page 4.

Chapter 7

"Quality Draws a Crowd" from "Breaking the Law, Blaine's Teaching Outlines," Session 3, page 1.

Chapter 13

"Effective Marketing" from "Breaking the Law, Blaine's Teaching Outlines," Session 3, page 4.

meet blaine bartel

Past: Came to Christ at age 16 on the heels of the Jesus movement. While in pursuit of a professional freestyle skiing career, answered God's call to reach young people. Developed and hosted groundbreaking television series, *Fire by Nite.* Planted and pastored a growing church in Colorado Springs.

Present: Serves under his pastor and mentor of nearly 20 years, Willie George, senior pastor of 12,000 member Church On The Move in Tulsa, OK. Youth pastor of Oneighty®, America's largest local church youth ministry, and reaching more than 1,500 students weekly. National director of Oneighty's® worldwide outreaches, including a network of over 400 affiliated youth ministries. Host of Elevate, one of the largest annual youth leadership training conferences in the nation. Host of Thrive™ youth leader audio resource series, listened to by thousands of youth leaders each month.

Passion: Summed up in three simple words, "Serving America's Future." Blaine's life quest is "to relevantly introduce the person of Jesus Christ to each new generation of young people, leaving footprints for future leaders to follow."

Personal: Still madly in love with his wife and partner of 20 years, Cathy. Raising 3 boys who love God, Jeremy—17, Dillon—15, and Brock—13. Avid hockey player and fan, with a rather impressive Gretzky memorabilia collection.

Additional copies of this book available from your local bookstore.

HARRISON HOUSE • Tulsa, OK 74153

To contact Blaine Bartel, write:

Blaine Bartel
Serving America's Future
P. O. Box 691923
Tulsa, OK 74169
www.blainebartel.com

Please include your prayer requests and comments when you write.

To contact Oneighty® write:
Oneighty® • P. O. Box 770 • Tulsa, OK 74101
www.oneighty.com

The Harrison House Vision

Proclaiming the truth and the power
Of the Gospel of Jesus Christ
With excellence;

Challenging Christians to
Live victoriously,
Grow spiritually,
Know God intimately.